The Origins of
the First World War

LANCASTER PAMPHLETS

The Origins of the First World War

Third edition

Ruth Henig

London and New York

First published 1989
by Routledge
11 New Fetter Lane, London EC4P 4EE

Simultaneously published in the USA and Canada
by Routledge
29 West 35th Street, New York, NY 10001

Second edition published 1993
Third edition published 2002

Routledge is an imprint of the Taylor & Francis Group

© 1989, 1993, 2002 Ruth Henig

Typeset in $10\frac{1}{2}$/12pt Bembo by RefineCatch Limited, Bungay, Suffolk
Printed and bound in Great Britain by
St Edmundsbury Press, Bury St Edmunds, Suffolk

British Library Cataloguing in Publication Data
A catalogue record for this book is available from the British Library

Library of Congress Cataloging in Publication Data
A catalog record for this book has been requested

ISBN 0–415–26185–6

Contents

Foreword

Lancaster Pamphlets offer concise and up-to-date accounts of major historical topics, primarily for the help of students preparing for Advanced Level examinations, though they should also be of value to those pursuing introductory courses in universities and other institutions of higher education. Without being all-embracing, their aims are to bring some of the central themes of problems confronting students and teachers into sharper focus than the textbook writer can hope to do; to provide the reader with some of the results of recent research which the textbook may not embody; and to stimulate thought about the whole interpretation of the topic under discussion.

At the end of this pamphlet is a list of works, most of them recent or fairly recent, which the writer considers most important for those who wish to study the subject further.

Introduction to the third edition

Students and general readers alike remain strongly interested in the causes, events and consequences of the First World War. The conflict is rightly seen as one of the major events – if not THE major event – which shaped the subsequent course of the 20th century not just in Europe but also in the wider world. Because its consequences were so profound, there is an enduring interest in how the conflict started and whether it could have been avoided.

The aim of this revised edition, therefore, is to guide students and general readers through the daunting collections of books and documents which continue to pour out in ever greater quantities on this topic. It is written in particular for those who have only a basic general knowledge of the diplomacy and crises of the early 20th century and who want to acquire a clearer overview of the major conflicts and sources of tension dividing Europe after 1900 and of why they resulted in the outbreak of war in August 1914.

The book is divided into two main sections. The first chapter examines the consequences of German unification after 1871 and the challenges which growing German economic and military power posed to the other great powers of Europe by 1900. It looks in particular at the diplomatic and military responses of France, Russia and Britain and at the formation of the Triple Entente which had emerged amongst these three powers by 1907 to counter-balance the Triple Alliance of Germany, Austria-Hungary and Italy which had been concluded in 1882.

The chapter also traces the growing problems in eastern and south-eastern Europe resulting from the decline in power of the Habsburg and Ottoman Empires, and the rise of serious tensions in the Balkan region which culminated in two Balkan wars in 1912–13. The chapter concludes by focusing on the chain of events triggered off by the assassination of Austrian archduke Franz Ferdinand in Sarajevo in June 1914 which resulted in the outbreak of a major war in Europe some six weeks later.

All historical events have complex and multiple causes, and this is especially true of the outbreak of the First World War. Whilst the first chapter seeks to identify the main issues which interacted so potently to bring about war, the second chapter looks at the ways in which successive generations of historians and commentators from different countries have interpreted the events and prioritised the factors which they argue were the main causes of war.

As we shall see, a fascinating historical debate has unfolded since the end of the First World War, with a great range of divergent views and perspectives emerging and being challenged in their turn by new interpretations. Thus the war has been depicted as the result of a chain of events spiralling out of control, as the inevitable consequence of the growth of new 'economic imperialism', as a result of competing alliance systems, as the outcome of incompatible nationalist ambitions and, more recently, as the result of planned and pre-emptive military aggression on the part of Austria-Hungary and of Germany. The aim of this second chapter is to consider these different interpretations, and to show how they have changed over time, influenced by subsequent events such as the outbreak of a second European conflict in 1939, and also by the emergence of new or hitherto unavailable documentary evidence.

Whilst in recent years the historical debate has focused heavily on German and Austro-Hungarian responsibility for precipitating war in 1914, prompted by the detailed research and writing of the German historian Professor Fritz Fischer and his research students in the 1960s and 1970s, new works contine to reveal fresh insights and different perspectives. I have taken the opportunity of this new edition to examine some of the most recent publications on the origins of the First World War, and to explain the approach and main conclusions of their authors. It is important for students to be aware of the ways in which the historical debate has unfolded since the Second World War, and the directions in which it is moving at the beginning of a new century. This will hopefully make it easier to assess the evidence available in the light of the ongoing debate and help students to formulate valid arguments and draw sound and informed conclusions, based on up-to-date information.

Of course there can never be a 'right' or 'wrong' answer to the question of why the Great War broke out when it did. But what we can all do is to contribute to the discussions and debates, try to understand the challenges and problems the main decision makers believed that they were facing in the years before 1914, and hope to learn some lessons from history which might be of benefit to us and to our successors. Thus a general aim of this book is to celebrate the rich diversity and endless fascination of history, and to stimulate a new generation of young people to study past events and think about the ways in which they have shaped the present and may guide the future. The aim of the annotated bibliography at the end of the book is to generate further discussion and to recommend a range of more detailed works which will supplement and expand upon the general account offered in this introductory work.

Acknowledgements

I would like to thank my colleagues, Professor Evans, Dr King and Professor Gooch for their valuable suggestions and help at crucial stages in the writing of this pamphlet. I would also like to take this opportunity to thank members of the Rendsburg and district SPD for their hospitality over the past fifteen years to their 'twin-town' Lancaster comrades, and for their willingness to discuss freely and frankly with me many contentious aspects of German and international history. I dedicate it to Jutta and to Ian in particular, and to international friendship in general.

Ruth Henig

The Balkans and the effects of the Balkan Wars

Europe in 1914

Timeline of key events

1871 unification of Germany and establishment of the German empire

1879 defensive alliance drawn up between Germany and Austria-Hungary

1882 Triple Alliance agreed between Germany, Austria-Hungary and Italy

1887 Triple Alliance renewed; Mediterranean agreements concluded between Britain, Austria-Hungary and Italy to maintain peace and the *status quo* in the Mediterranean region and the Near East

Reinsurance Treaty signed between Germany and Russia

1890 Bismark departs from office, having been Chancellor in the new empire since 1871

1894 France and Russia sign a defensive alliance

1898, 1900 German Navy Laws establish basis for a powerful German battle fleet

1902 Anglo-Japanese alliance concluded

1904 France and Britain sign agreement relating to colonial matters, which becomes known as the *Entente Cordiale*

1905 First Moroccan crisis. Wilhelm II intervenes in Moroccan affairs hoping to drive Britain and France apart, but fails

1906 January Algeciras conference settles Moroccan crisis. Britain and France hold military talks, including possibility of a British expeditionary force being sent to France in the event of a military conflict

February Britain launches the *Dreadnought*, a big gun battleship which makes existing naval vessels obsolete. Naval rivalry intensifies between Britain and Germany

1907 Britain and Russia sign a convention; France and Russia now referred to as the Triple Entente powers

1908 Austria-Hungary annexes the former Turkish provinces of Bosnia and Herzegovina

1911 Second Moroccan crisis when German gunboat *Panther* arrives at Agadir. Crisis is resolved by the autumn in talks between Germany and France

Italy declares war on Turkey and annexes Tripoli in Libya

1912 First Balkan War breaks out with Greece, Serbia, Bulgaria and Montenegro fighting against Turkey; Turkey is defeated

1913 Second Balkan War breaks out when Greece and Serbia fight against their former ally Bulgaria

1914 28 June Archduke Franz Ferdinand assassinated at Sarajevo in Bosnia, by a Bosnian extremist trained and equipped in Serbia

5 July Austria-Hungary assured of full German support for military action against Serbia

23 July Austria-Hungary sends Serbia a ten-point ultimatum

24 July Russia declares support for Serbia in the event of attack by Austria-Hungary

25 July Serbia accepts most, but not all, points of the ultimatum. Austria-Hungary begins mobilisation

28 July Austria-Hungary declares war on Serbia

30 July Russia declares general mobilisation

1 August Germany declares war on Russia; France mobilises

3 August Germany declares war on France and invades Belgium

4 August Germany declares war on Belgium; Britain declares war on Germany

5 August Austria-Hungary declares war on Russia

10 August France declares war on Austria-Hungary

12 August Britain declares war on Austria-Hungary

1
The origins of war

Introduction

Europe, in the early months of 1914, seemed to be at peace. Sir Winston Churchill, writing in the 1920s, recalled that 'the spring and summer of 1914 were marked in Europe by an exceptional tranquility'. Anglo-German relations, after years of tense naval rivalry, seemed to be improving as the two powers negotiated amicably about the possible future disposition of the Portuguese colonial empire in Africa. French bitterness towards Germany, centred on the 'lost provinces' of Alsace and Lorraine, appeared to be abating. Austria–Hungary and Russia had refused to allow their Balkan 'clients' to draw them into war in 1912 and 1913.

But this picture of reduced tensions and of increasing stability amongst Europe's great powers was illusory. It masked great underlying problems and increasing pessimism on the part of many European leaders about developments which they believed were undermining their countries' position and great power status. Since 1900, Europe had been wracked by a series of crises, each of which had brought her great powers closer to war. These crises were provoked by a number of serious issues which were causing mounting friction amongst the powers and which, by 1914, in the opinion of many European statesmen, were becoming insoluble by means other than resort to war.

A number of historians have traced the roots of the conflicts and antagonisms of this period back through the previous forty years. The titles of recent books on the origins of the First World War, such as *The Long Fuse* by Lafore and *The Collapse of the Concert of Europe* by Langhorne emphasize the long-term factors which were slowly but inexorably undermining the foundations of European stability.

The outcome of the Franco-Prussian war of 1870–1 and the establishment of a new German Empire which included the two former French provinces of Alsace and Lorraine decisively altered the distribution of power in Europe. The enormous expansion of the German economy after unification and the accompanying growth of German political ambitions – particularly after the period of Bismarck's chancellorship – caused considerable alarm to the other European powers. At the same time, rapid industrialization and urbanization were generating social and economic conflicts in most European countries and were widening the arena of political debate and participation. The spread of strong nationalist feelings, which had helped to bring about Italian and German unification and were now at work in eastern Europe and in the Balkans, made it more difficult for governments to compromise on their stated national objectives and to pursue flexible strategies of diplomacy. This was increasingly evident in the Near East and in the Balkans where the decline of the Ottoman Empire triggered off amongst the great powers a scramble for concessions and for influence made more dangerous and potentially explosive by the accompanying release of Balkan nationalism. While Russia sought to profit from Turkey's weakness, Austria-Hungary tried to prevent the expansion of Russian power, and Germany, France and Britain attempted with varying degrees of success to bolster up Turkey, the 'sick man of Europe', and to contain Austro-Russian hostility.

The rise of German power after 1870, the corresponding relative decline of France particularly in terms of economic strength and size of population, the increasing weakness of the Ottoman Empire and the unending conflicts between the two ramshackle empires of eastern Europe, Austria-Hungary and Russia, all contributed to a lengthy period of unsettled and at times stormy international diplomacy. Many European statesmen of the 1870s and 1880s expected a major war to break out in the near future; indeed, so concerned was Bismarck about this possibility that he concentrated a large part of his considerable abilities after 1871 on the establishment of a complicated diplomatic network of understandings which would secure European peace and stability. In the short term he was successful, but as we shall see, his policies had long-term repercussions which helped to undermine the post-1871 European settlement he had done so much to establish.

Bismarck's legacy

The unification of Germany and establishment of the German Empire in 1871 clearly altered the distribution of power within Europe and ushered in a new international order. But what was most significant about the new German Empire was its internal power structure and the circumstances in which it was established. The federation of German states which made up the new united Germany was dominated by Prussia. The constitution was carefully drawn up to maximize Prussian power and Prussian interests. And within Prussia social control and political power had traditionally been exercised, and continued to be exercised, by the *Junkers*, a class of nobility who owned large landed estates and operated within a neo-feudal social structure. They owed military and political allegiance to the Prussian king – who became after 1871 the German Kaiser – and ruled autocratically over the classes beneath them. Bismarck himself came from a prominent *Junker* family, and according to A. J. P. Taylor his foreign policy was 'always shaped by "Junker" needs'. One could indeed argue that Bismarck's *Junker* background influenced all his policies, especially after he became Chancellor in the new united Germany in 1871. Bismarck sought to preserve the traditional Prussian social and political order and to enshrine it in the new German Empire. The forces released by industrialization and urbanization could not be allowed to undermine *Junker* power, and for nearly twenty years Bismarck struggled to keep liberalism, socialism and democracy at bay. Abroad Bismarck's concern was also the preservation of order, but in this case a newly-established European order created after Prussia's defeat of France.

Bismarck's objective after 1871 was to stabilize Europe around the new German Empire. France's inevitable desire for revenge and for the return of Alsace and Lorraine was to be countered by depriving her of European allies through skilful diplomacy, and by encouraging her to embark on colonial expansion in Africa and Asia which could have the added advantage of embroiling her in conflict with Great

3

Britain. Meanwhile, Austria-Hungary and Russia had to be brought together with Germany in some diplomatic alignment to preserve order in eastern Europe. Bismarck achieved this in 1872 through a meeting in Berlin of the emperors of the three monarchies, but it was in practice very difficult for the three rulers to reach agreement on anything very concrete. All the 'League of the Three Emperors' actually achieved was a ringing declaration against revolution in general and against the Marxist International in particular – an international movement of workers' associations and socialist revolutionaries which was at the time more concerned with its own internal squabbles over ideological purity than with thrusting forward a significant revolutionary challenge. Through the isolation of France and the League of the Three Emperors, Bismarck hoped to be able to contain the new currents of nationalism and industrialism which were flowing so strongly through Europe from west to east. His chief difficulty, however, lay in keeping Russia and Austria-Hungary in harness, pulling alongside Germany. The two great east European empires had conflicting interests, particularly in the Balkans area where, as Turkey continued to decline in power, former Turkish provinces in south-east Europe struggled for national identity and for independence.

The problems in south-east Europe in the late 19th century

Some of these provinces contained sizeable communities of Slav people who appealed to the Russian Emperor on grounds of race and religion to assist them in their historic struggle against the Turks. Panslavism, a crusading movement of support for Slav ambitions in the Balkans and Near East, swept through Russia in the mid-nineteenth century and aroused such strong sentiments amongst the Orthodox Russian parts of the population that even in autocratic Russia no ruler could ignore their force. But while Russia was being pulled into the Balkans, the Austrians were determined to try to minimize Russian involvement, dampen down national and independence movements and shore up the Turkish Empire as far as possible. As the Austro-Hungarian foreign minister, Andrassy, presented the situation to the Habsburg Crown council in 1875.

Turkey possesses a utility almost providential for Austria-Hungary. For Turkey maintains the status quo of the small Balkan states and impedes their aspirations. If it were not for Turkey, all these aspirations would fall down on our heads ... if Bosnia-Hercegovina should go to Serbia or Montenegro, or if a new state should be formed there which we cannot prevent then we should be ruined and should ourselves assume the role of the 'Sick Man'.

Russia and Austria-Hungary were therefore in headlong conflict over their policy in south-east Europe and this was clearly revealed in the period between 1875 and 1878, when a series of anti-Turkish revolts swept through the Balkans and threatened the integrity of the Ottoman Empire. It was not possible for Bismarck to support both Russia and Austria-Hungary and when he could not force the two powers to work together or to reach a compromise over their differences he chose to work more closely with Austria-Hungary since any drastic decline in her position, which could follow a Turkish collapse, would imperil Bismarck's whole strategy of great power conservation. Russia, as the champion of the Balkan Slavs, was left to challenge Turkish power alone and was unable to win a decisive military victory. But the Russo-Turkish war of 1877 did have the result of further weakening Turkey's hold on her European provinces in the Balkans, thereby making it even more difficult for Bismarck to try to maintain a stable balance between Austria-Hungary and Russia in south-east Europe. The Congress of Berlin in 1878 tried to demarcate Balkan spheres of interest, with Austria-Hungary in the west occupying Bosnia and Hercegovina and garrisoning a small strip of Turkish territory – the Sanjak of Novibazar – between the newly-created states of Serbia and Montenegro, and Russia in the east recovering a part of Bessarabia and gaining the port of Batum on the Black Sea. But Austro-Russian rivalry could not be contained for long by such means, and Bismarck was fearful that the Austrian government might seek French support to strengthen its diplomatic and military position.

The formation of the Triple Alliance 1879–1882

In 1879 he made the fateful decision to conclude a defensive alliance between Germany and Austria-Hungary, in a move calculated to maintain French diplomatic isolation and to force Austrian co-operation with Russia. This second objective was underlined in 1881 when for the second time a League of the Three Emperors was

5

constituted, this time an alliance to preserve the stability of the Near East and to pledge neutrality if one of the three empires came to be involved in war with a fourth power.

Having bound Germany, Austria-Hungary and Russia together, Bismarck now drew in Italy. In 1882, a Triple Alliance was concluded between Austria-Hungary, Germany and Italy and the preamble of the treaty outlined its objective 'to increase the guarantees of general peace, to strengthen the monarchical principle, and by that to assure the maintenance of social and political order in their respective states'. At the same time, France was encouraged to pursue her colonial ambitions in Africa. As a result of a serious nationalist uprising in Egypt which threatened the security of both European financial interests and the Suez Canal, Britain sought French assistance to establish a joint occupation of the country. When the French government failed to reply, British troops marched in alone and established a British protectorate in 1882. Bismarck capitalized on this situation by encouraging French claims for compensation elsewhere in Africa. He also ventured into the African arena himself over the next two years and laid claim on behalf of Germany to areas of land bordering on British spheres of influence and trade – South West Africa, Togoland and the Cameroons, and East Africa. This proved to be a very popular policy within Germany, but was undertaken by Bismarck for reasons of diplomatic gain rather than as a result of domestic or colonial pressures. Bismarck was not slow to see the advantages of constructing a colonial understanding between Germany and France at Britain's expense which would make it easier for France to accept her loss of status in Europe as a result of the acquisition of a great colonial empire in Africa. But Bismarck's interest in African conquest was fleeting; after 1885 it was not seriously pursued. As he commented, 'my map of Africa lies in Europe. Here lies Russia and here lies France, and we are in the middle. That is my map of Africa'. Bismarck was not interested in pursuing a world policy for Germany as a first priority. His concern was German security and dominance in Europe.

In 1887 his network of agreements was widened when Britain and Italy agreed to co-operate in maintaining the status quo in the Mediterranean. In the same year, the Triple Alliance was renewed, Austria-Hungary and Germany made new separate treaties with Italy and Austria-Hungary associated herself with the Anglo-Italian agreement. In December 1887 there was a second 'Mediterranean' agreement between Britain, Austria–Hungary and Italy in which the three powers undertook to maintain peace and the status quo in the Near East, the freedom of the Straits, Turkish authority in Asia Minor and Turkish suzerainty in Bulgaria. Moreover Germany and Russia had also signed an agreement in the same year, commonly referred to as the Reinsurance Treaty, defining the circumstances in which they would remain neutral in a conflict involving the other power.

The results of Bismarck's diplomacy

By the time of his departure from office in 1890, Bismarck had secured his diplomatic objectives in Europe. France was still isolated, though in 1888, in a significant move, a Russian loan was floated on the French money markets and a year later the Russians placed a large order for French rifles. Agreements had been concluded with both Austria–Hungary and Russia, and a Mediterranean compact covered Italy and Great Britain. These were great achievements on Bismarck's part which ensured short-term European stability and have led many historians to conclude that Europe's problems became acute only after Bismarck's fall. However one can argue very strongly that both Bismarck's diplomatic strategy between 1871 and 1890 and his tactics bequeathed serious long-term problems for his successors.

No network of diplomatic agreements, however elaborate, could extinguish France's resentment over her defeat in war, her loss of territory, and the manner in which she had been outmanoeuvred by Bismarck both militarily and diplomatically. Bismarck was well aware after 1871 that French hostility towards the new German Empire would be enduring, and that French rulers would exploit any opportunity to try to overturn the new European power structure. At the same time, Bismarck's alliance with Austria–Hungary inevitably alienated Russia and paved the way for a Franco-Russian understanding which could easily harden into an alliance. It is undoubtedly the case that Bismarck worked very hard to keep Russia aligned to Germany, but the very scale of his efforts indicates the difficulty he faced in trying to keep France and Russia apart, once he opted to conclude a binding agreement with Austria–Hungary in 1879. Furthermore, the protection of *Junker* agriculture in East Prussia by tariffs hit at Russian grain exports to Germany and increased the importance to Russia of French financial and commercial assistance. The Austro-German agreement itself was a dubious asset to Germany. Bismarck had hoped to use it to try to keep Austro-Russian rivalry in check and to prevent Austria–Hungary from concluding destabilizing agreements with other powers. It was to be a mechanism through which Germany could control Austrian foreign policy. But it could also be used by a declining Austria–Hungary to drag Germany into the south-east European minefield and to force her to agree to military assistance against Russia. It limited German diplomatic options and the short-term stability it yielded turned very quickly to long-term inflexibility and the tense situation of two European alliance systems confronting each other menacingly.

Bismarck's African ventures also had undesirable long-term consequences. Britain was cast as the villain of the colonial drama, jealously guarding vast tracts of tropical lands and spitefully denying Germany her rightful share of the spoils. The German public was given the impression that German claims to colonies had been thwarted when in fact Bismarck had laid the basis for a sizeable German Empire in the mid-1880s and could have negotiated, had he so wished, to expand and develop it systematically. As we have seen, his priorities lay firmly in Europe, and thus Germany's appetite for worldwide influence and for an empire was whetted without being in any way satisfied. Bismarck's cynical manipulation of public pressures within Germany and his calculated exploitation of diplomatic incidents and crises for political and military gain were methods which would provoke serious international confrontation in less skilful hands. Ultimately his overriding objective, which was shared fully by the Kaiser and by his successors, was to perpetuate and to expand *Junker* and Prussian power within Germany and within Europe. His very success in the pursuit of this aim between 1871 and 1890, and in particular the tactics he employed, contributed greatly to the increasing tensions within Germany and within Europe.

The challenge of German power

After unification in 1871, the power of Germany increased spectacularly. Her population leapt from 41 million in 1870 to over 66 million in 1914, and while one-third of those employed worked in agriculture, almost 40 per cent worked in the rapidly expanding industrial sector. Coal production had increased over the period by 800 per cent and had almost caught up with the British volume of output by 1914. More electricity was generated than in Britain, Italy and France combined. In steel production, German furnaces turned out two-thirds of the European total. This was of course a greater quantity than Germany's main rivals, Britain, France and Russia, put together. German electric and chemical industries led the world in their inventiveness and in the quality of their products.

Such a dramatic economic expansion was bound to be viewed with alarm by Germany's neighbours, and in particular by France. The Prussian defeat of France in the war of 1870–1 had laid the foundations for this rapid German growth, and much of it was based in the former French provinces of Alsace and Lorraine. We have seen that it was not politically possible for any French government after 1871 publicly to renounce the prospect of one day being in a position to regain these two provinces. Equally, successive German governments framed their diplomatic and military plans on the assumption that France would seek to profit from any crisis involving Germany by invading Alsace and Lorraine. Up to 1890, Bismarck had succeeded in minimizing this threat by keeping France diplomatically isolated, but his successors lacked his diplomatic skills and were not able to continue successfully his strategy of French containment in Europe. By 1892 republican and Catholic France had managed to conclude a military alliance with autocratic and Orthodox Russia, which was ratified in late 1893. In addition to mutual military support if either power were attacked by Germany, the agreement furnished Russia with much needed French capital for industrial and railway development. Between 1899 and 1914, 25 per cent of France's considerable sums of foreign investment went to Russia.

German industrial expansion and military strength in the first decade of the twentieth century were clearly a threat to both the French and Russian governments, and they tried to catch up with their neighbour in industrial output and in military technology and development. But the gap continued to widen alarmingly. France's population remained stagnant at around 39 million, and the development of her industries was slow and patchy. By 1910, Germany produced three times as much iron as France, four times as much steel and seven times as much coal.

Russia's population expanded to 140 million in European Russia by 1914, and the country underwent considerable industrialization from the 1890s, benefiting greatly from foreign investment. She became the fourth greatest industrialized power behind Britain, Germany and the United States, and overtook her French ally in coal, iron and steel production. Even so, her coal production by 1912 was only 13 per cent of Germany's, her pig iron production 23 per cent and her steel output 26 per cent. In other words, Germany dominated continental Europe economically by 1914. As A. J. P. Taylor has pointed out, she was close to securing peacefully the economic mastery of Europe. This dominance in turn was bound to give her a strong military position, both in terms of the quality and quantity of weaponry she could produce and in terms of the considerable army she could deploy in the heart of Europe. In addition, as we have seen, the German Empire had been allied to Austria-Hungary since 1879 and to Italy since 1882. Thus central, eastern and south-east Europe was dominated by a German-Austrian 'bloc', increasing in population and economic strength, which threatened to destroy completely any semblance of a European 'balance of power'.

Anglo-German economic and naval rivalry

This development was bound to cause alarm not just to France and Russia but to the great British Empire as well. Britain was isolated to some degree from developments on the European mainland, and in the late-nineteenth century was concentrating on the consolidation of her vast worldwide empire and the expansion of overseas trade. In 1890 Britain possessed more registered tonnage than the rest of the world put together, and London was the undisputed financial capital of the world. But industrialization first in the United States and then in Germany threatened Britain's industrial and commercial supremacy, especially when it became clear that their increases in productivity were far outstripping those of Britain. The use of tariffs to protect home industries hit British exports, and there was growing competition amongst the great powers for raw materials and for markets in Africa, South America and the Far and Near East.

With economic rivalry went a struggle for political concessions and for imperial possessions, a struggle in which Britain found herself very much on the defensive, particularly against France and Germany. Britain's naval strength and her ability to protect vital sea communications were further threatened by the Franco-Russian alliance which brought together Europe's second and third strongest naval powers. From the late 1890s, also, she had to face an even more dangerous naval challenge – from Germany.

German leaders believed very passionately by the turn of the century that their country was not gaining as large a share of colonial possessions as its economic strength and great power status merited. As the German Chancellor Bulow declared in the German Parliament, or *Reichstag*, in 1897, 'we don't want to put anyone else in the shade, but we too demand a place in the sun'. Since Britain possessed by far the greatest extent of overseas territory and influence at the time, it followed that German concessions would have to be wrested largely from a reluctant Britain. There was considerable jealousy and hostility within German ruling circles towards Britain and towards what were seen as her ridiculous imperial, economic and political pretensions, though these feelings were tinged with admiration as well. The Kaiser and his advisers desperately wanted Germany to be a world power on the same scale as Britain, but to achieve this they believed that British naval mastery would first have to be challenged. This was the aim of Tirpitz's naval policy.

The construction of a German navy in the late 1890s fulfilled many objectives for the authoritarian and militaristic German state. It gratified the Kaiser's wish to build up a German navy which would be the equal of Britain's. It supplied a steady market for the expanding iron and steel works of the Ruhr and of Upper Silesia. It provided tangible proof of growing German power, which could rouse the patriotism of the German population and serve as a unifying force to overcome social tensions in a way which could no longer be achieved in an age of mass politics by the élitist and aristocratic Prussian army officer corps. But most important of all, naval construction symbolized Germany's intention to become a leading world power and to take a full part in world affairs, demanding her fair share of colonial spoils and imperial concessions. The Navy Laws of 1898 and 1900 laid the basis for a powerful German battle fleet prepared to take action in the North Sea and conceived primarily as a force which would deter Britain from taking any hostile action against Germany. Even though the British fleet would be considerably stronger than the German one in the foreseeable future, any attempt by Britain to attack the German fleet or to threaten Germany's economic power by a blockade of the European mainland in a crisis would lead to a mighty naval clash which would be bound to leave the British navy severely weakened. Thus the Germans reasoned that a strong German battle fleet would force Britain to acquiesce in Germany's new world power status and might even induce her to come to an agreement, which would further strengthen Germany's position.

The Anglo-French entente

The German naval strategy proved totally misconceived as an instrument for securing increased world recognition and power. Not only did it arouse Britain's fierce antagonism but it strengthened the forces of opposition to German ambitions in Europe. To meet the potential European challenges to her naval domination at the turn of the century, Britain withdrew her naval squadrons from the Caribbean and concluded an alliance with Japan in 1902. The German Navy Laws, and impending hostilities between France's ally, Russia, and Britain's new ally, Japan, in Manchuria and Korea led Britain and France to seek an agreement which would prevent them from being drawn into the conflict on opposite sides. The resulting Anglo-French entente of 1904 was largely a colonial agreement, settling long-standing differences in Newfoundland, Siam, the New Hebrides and North Africa. In particular, the two powers agreed to recognize Morocco as primarily a French sphere of influence and Egypt as primarily a British one.

The entente secured its initial objective when Russia and Japan became involved in a war in the Far East between 1904 and 1905. Britain and France stood aside as Russia suffered a series of humiliating defeats at the hands of Japan. Domestic unrest and financial weakness forced Russia to the negotiating table in 1905, and it was to be many years before her armed forces recovered their operational strength. More importantly, the revolutionary upheavals which had broken out with such force in St Petersburg and in Moscow in 1905 shook the confidence of the Tsar's court and forced Nicholas II into a series of constitutional and political reforms. After 1905, the Russian government faced a painful dilemma. An aggressive foreign policy stance would serve to restore Russian prestige abroad and to unify disparate elements in the empire in a patriotic fervour at home, but any outbreak of war itself was likely to bring revolution and disintegration.

The German government was fully aware of Russia's internal difficulties and hoped to exploit them to expand German influence in central and south-east Europe. At the same time Germany felt menaced by the new Anglo-French agreement and decided to challenge it at an early stage in an effort to drive apart the two powers and possibly to secure from Britain a pledge of neutrality in the event of a European war. In March 1905 the Kaiser, who was *en route* for a cruise in the Mediterranean, was induced by his ministers to stop off at

Tangiers to pay his respects to the Sultan of Morocco. The visit was intended to serve as a demonstration that Morocco could count on German help against French expansion, and the Germans hoped that they might gain British support as well. The visit inevitably sparked off an international crisis which dragged on through the summer. But the result was not the breakup of the *entente*, as the Germans had hoped, but the strengthening of ties between Britain and France and the consolidation of France's position in Morocco. The British government resented Germany's bullying tactics and was alarmed at Germany's continuing naval build-up. Two years later, in 1907, Britain concluded an understanding with her great nineteenth-century rival for Asian influence, Russia. The two powers agreed to regulate their spheres of influence and concessions in Afghanistan, Persia and Tibet.

Triple Entente against Triple Alliance

Thus by the end of 1907, a Triple Entente had come into being, facing a Triple Alliance of Germany, Austria-Hungary and Italy. Furthermore, Britain was responding to the German naval challenge both by increasing the rate of her own naval construction and also by designing a revolutionary new battleship, the dreadnought, which rendered obsolete all previous models. The German government was finding it more and more difficult to finance the naval construction programme and, what was worse, the naval race, far from promoting Germany's rise to world power status, was blocking it. A second attempt by Germany to exploit the Moroccan situation, by sending the German gunboat *Panther* to Agadir in 1911, was also a failure, but not before it had, in Churchill's words, set 'all alarm bells throughout Europe' quivering. This second Moroccan crisis drove the British and French military and naval advisers to more serious planning. In 1912 a naval agreement was reached between the two powers whereby the British fleet was to undertake the defence of the Channel and France's Atlantic coastline, while the French navy moved into the Mediterranean.

By 1912, Germany's leaders not only felt that German world ambitions had been thwarted but perceived her European position to be increasingly vulnerable. The naval race with Britain had been lost. Russia was recovering from the military reverses and revolutionary challenges of 1904–5, and had embarked on a process of military reorganisation. The aim was to enable her considerable forces to be concentrated and mobilised much more quickly than had previously been the case. Yet despite this growing challenge in the east, Austria-Hungary threatened to drag her into Balkan conflict and into confrontation with Russia. Successive German attempts to detach Russia from France or to drive a wedge between France and Britain had failed. Britain had not been driven to seek an alliance with Germany or to promise her neutrality in a European conflict. Italy's support was becoming less and less reliable, as her ambitions were coming increasingly into conflict with those of Austria-Hungary.

German domestic problems

At home, industrialization and urbanization had created a large, restless working class which increasingly looked to the German Social Democratic Party to champion its interests. Though the German *Reichstag* had strictly limited powers, regular elections and universal manhood suffrage offered to politicians of the centre and the left an opportunity to campaign for liberal and socialist policies. Since the Prussian-dominated German government refused to implement any political or economic reforms which might undermine the Prussian *Junker* supremacy in Germany, and since they had secured the support of the German industrialists and middle classes for policies of agricultural support and tariffs which drove up the price of everyday commodities and in particular bread, working-class hostility grew. In the 1912 *Reichstag* elections, the Social Democratic Party secured over one-third of the votes cast. With political concessions out of the question, many extreme nationalists and army officers began to talk of an impending civil war and to dream of a dramatic military coup which would smash the forces of the left and pave the way for German military conquests abroad. The German government felt itself to be under siege both at home and abroad, with its freedom for manoeuvre rapidly disappearing.

German leaders by 1912 felt impelled to propose a substantial army increase together with an increase in naval strength. Though the *Reichstag* agreed to fund these programmes, a majority of deputies insisted that the costs should be met partly by the introduction of a wealth tax, which was bound to cause great social antagonism on the part of the upper classes. Within a year, further military increases were put into effect, leading to the greatest peacetime addition in numbers in the army's history. Its strength rose by 30 per cent to 665,000, with plans for further increases in numbers to over three quarters of a million in 1914.

Not surprisingly, this German move provoked the entente powers into reviewing their own military strength. In 1913, the French government authorized the extension of military conscription from two to three years, the aim being to give France a force of about 700,000 men. The Russian government, which had put the bulk of defence spending into naval expansion since 1906, in a great programme to re-equip the Black Sea and Baltic fleets, now switched attention to the army. A four-year programme was put in train designed to bring about a 40 per cent increase in the size of the peacetime army by 1917, with increased artillery efficiency to bring the Russian firing capacity to German levels. In addition, British military planners were discussing with their French counterparts plans to send a British expeditionary force to France if she was the unprovoked victim of aggression by a hostile power.

While some details of these military arrangements remained secret, the broad outlines and implications were well known and provided the basis for the calculations of military planners about future needs. Europe by 1914 was experiencing a spiralling arms race, and it fuelled Germany's fears for her future. Every move she made to consolidate her position provoked countermoves which left her seemingly in a worse position. The sense of despondency and frustration experienced by German leaders was reinforced by the difficulty of finding markets for a growing volume of exports. Some German industrialists were suggesting that what Germany needed was a central European customs union, a vast *Mitteleuropa*, protected by tariff walls, which could supply her with a steady supply of vital raw materials and furnish outlets for her goods at terms favourable to German trade.

Until this could become a reality, the German government switched its attention to the Near East and to the possibility of building up a sphere of influence in the Turkish Empire. German capital competed with French in the scramble for concessions to finance a projected Berlin to Baghdad railway. In November 1913, Captain Liman von Sanders was despatched at the head of a German military mission to Turkey. The Kaiser, in bidding farewell to the party, hoped that through their efforts, 'the German flag will soon fly over the fortifications of the Bosphorus'. The announcement that the Turks had appointed von Sanders to command the first Ottoman Army Corps in Constantinople sent shudders through the Russian court, where it was seen as a triumph for German efforts to cultivate close ties with the Sultan and thus be in a position to block historical and strategic Russian interests in the Dardanelles and the Near East. This area was of increasing economic concern to the Russians: between 1903 and 1912, 37 per cent of their exports and threequarters of their grain shipments passed through the Straits. The Russians contemplated diplomatic and military measures against Turkey, conscious that these could lead to confrontation with Germany. In the event, the Germans agreed to a compromise, and von Sanders gave up his command of the Constantinople corps, to become instead Inspector-General of the Turkish army.

The threat of Russia

By 1914, German civilian and military leaders alike felt that their ambitions were being thwarted on all sides, while their rivals were increasing in strength and seemed ever more closely aligned. The Germans felt themselves to be encircled by the *entente* powers who were perceived to be tightening their grip on their enemies. In particular, the prospect of Russia's being able to harness her vast economic potential and mineral wealth haunted them. The German chancellor, Bethmann Hollweg, saw the future belonging to Russia which 'grows and grows and weighs upon us like a nightmare'. In 1912 he confessed to a friend that only 'a good deal of trust in God' and the hope of 'a Russian revolution' allowed him to sleep at night. Military leaders were particularly concerned about the growth of Russian strategic railways in Poland, for the construction of which French capital was being expressly provided. The German military response to the Franco–Russian alliance of 1892 had been to construct a plan, named after General Schlieffen, whereby in the event of Germany's being involved in hostilities, her armies would aim to deliver a rapid knockout blow against the French army, initially leaving only small numbers of troops to guard the frontier against Russia. Since the Russian military authorities needed about a month to mobilize and organize their troops for battle, this would give the Germans just enough time – if they invaded France in a broad sweep through Holland and Belgium and took the French army by surprise – to defeat France and then transfer their troops to the Eastern front. But speed was of the essence. If Russia could mobilize her troops within two or at the most three weeks, and if she were able to mobilize a greater proportion of her male population than hitherto and arm them adequately with modern weapons, the success of the Schlieffen plan would be highly uncertain. The plan had already been rendered considerably more risky by an adaptation to the plan in 1911, whereby Germany would respect Dutch neutrality and rely instead on capturing the Belgian fortress of Liège at an early stage of hostilities. That would enable the German army to pass large numbers of soldiers speedily through the four lines of railway track which ran south from Liège through the Belgian plain. If there were any hitches in the proceedings Germany might be left wide open to invasion from Russian troops in the east. A further possible drawback was that an unprovoked German invasion of neutral Belgium would greatly increase the risk of British military intervention. Not surprisingly, therefore, growing Russian industrialization and modernization was causing considerable alarm in Berlin, and was giving rise to plans for preventive war against France and Russia, to enable Germany to break out of its encirclement before it was too late. At a war council in December 1912 the Kaiser and his service chiefs held a thorough review of Germany's capacity to wage war against the *entente* powers, and army leaders were adamant that because of the alarming growth in Russian power, Russia should be attacked by Germany 'the sooner the better'. Plans were drawn up to widen the Kiel Canal to enable it to convey battleships from the Baltic to the North Sea, to bring army plans to a state of readiness for war, and to launch a press and propaganda campaign against Russia. By 1914, the idea of a preventive war seemed not only desirable but essential to many German leaders, as a result of Austria-Hungary's glaring inability to check growing Russian and Serbian influence in the Balkans. William II commented about a Russian newspaper article in June 1914 that if anyone doubted that Russia and France were 'preparing to attack Germany, he belongs in the lunatic asylum'.

The Balkans crisis

Both Austria-Hungary and Russia were multinational empires which had expanded over the centuries as a result of a combination of military victory, diplomatic negotiation and marriage settlement. Over one hundred languages were spoken in the vast Russian Empire, which stretched across nearly one-sixth of the world's land surface, and Russian nationals constituted less than half of the population. In

17

Austria–Hungary, at least fifteen different languages were regularly used, and the German-speaking population struggled to maintain its supremacy against the challenges of ten other racial groups. The forces of liberalism and nationalism which spread so powerfully through Europe in the nineteenth century threatened to weaken both states by undermining the absolute powers of the rulers and by feeding the nationalist sentiments of the different groups of subject peoples. The Habsburg Empire had already bowed to Hungarian pressure for autonomy in 1867, and faced increasing demands for greater rights and freedoms from Czechs and Southern Slavs. Both empires faced the same dilemma; modernization and industrialization were necessary to maintain military power, existing national frontiers and great power status, but both processes created opportunities for minority peoples such as Poles, Jews, Czechs and Serbs to secure an education and to increase their influence. Both governments, by the end of the nineteenth century, felt themselves to be under pressure both at home and abroad, and both in consequence were determined to act with resolution to protect what they regarded as vital national objectives. In some regions, their objectives clashed violently and neither power was prepared to see its influence weakened to the profit of the other.

Russia was concerned above all to secure an unobstructed outlet for her ships from the Black Sea through the Dardanelles and to establish political influence and, ultimately, eventual military control of Constantinople. Strategic and military considerations were reinforced here by the substantially increased volume of Russian exports, particularly grain, passing through the Straits every year. She was also concerned with the security of the borders of her vast empire in Central Asia and the Far East which lay open to attack from Persia, Afghanistan, India and Manchuria/Mongolia. Furthermore, as the staunch upholder of Russian Orthodox traditions and as protector of the Slav heritage, the Russian Tsar also regarded himself as bearing the full responsibility for the fate of the Balkan peoples who might turn to him in the face of attack by the Moslem Turks or the Catholic and predominantly German Habsburgs.

The decline of Turkey

The Habsburg Empire itself was concerned to hold together its territorial possessions and to maintain its position as a great European power. This was becoming increasingly difficult, not just because of the growing nationalist pressures inside Austria-Hungary but also because of the inability of the Turkish Empire to maintain control of its European subjects. The nineteenth century witnessed a succession of crises triggered off by Turkey's decline into 'the sick man of Europe', and each one threatened to bring Austria-Hungary and Russia into military conflict. Both countries sought to profit from Turkey's weakness and at the same time to minimize the threat of growing Balkan nationalism to their internal stability. In 1878, as we have seen, Austria-Hungary took administrative control of the two Turkish Balkan provinces of Bosnia and Hercegovina. Russia worked to strengthen her position in the eastern Balkans and at Constantinople. Both powers attempted to stabilize the situation in the Balkans and the Near East to their own advantage, but as Turkey grew ever weaker, the ambitions of the Balkan states grew stronger and threatened to destabilize the entire region and the Habsburg Empire as well.

The ambitions of one Balkan state in particular, Serbia, were of increasing concern to Austria-Hungary. The rulers of Serbia dreamed of one day uniting all Serbs and Croats in a greater Serbia, which might recreate the triumphs of its thirteenth-century namesake. Union with Bosnia, which had been a part of the old Serbia before the time of Ottoman conquest, was particularly desired. Since there were twice as many Serbs in the Habsburg Empire and in Bosnia and Hercegovina (7,300,000) as there were in Serbia itself (3,300,000), Serbian ambitions could only be realized at the expense of the territorial unity of the Habsburg Empire, opening the way for the ambitions of other subject nationalities, and it was hardly surprising, therefore, that Serbia was feared by the Habsburg rulers as a second Piedmont. Until 1903, under the rule of the pro-Austrian Obrenovic dynasty, Serbia was almost a satellite state of Austria-Hungary, but in that year the regime was brutally overthrown, and replaced by that of the pro-Russian Karageorgevics.

Serbian rivalry with Austria-Hungary

This change brought about a period of great antagonism between Serbia and Austria-Hungary, as Serbian national consciousness and ambitions grew. Austria-Hungary tried to bring economic pressure to bear on the landlocked state by means of the 'pig war', whereby

Serbian agricultural products were denied access to Austrian markets. Serbia, however, found other European outlets for its pigs and farm exports, and concentrated on spreading its influence in the southern part of the Habsburg territories and in Bosnia and Hercegovina. The inexorable decline of the Ottoman Empire was likely to offer Serbia considerable scope, and in a bid to contain Serbian expansion Austria–Hungary moved to annex Bosnia and Hercegovina formally in 1908. This action had been discussed with the Russian foreign minister, Isvolsky, who had given his agreement in exchange for Austria–Hungary using her good offices to secure for Russia greater influence at Constantinople and the right to free passage for Russian ships through the Straits in times of peace and war. However, other powers, especially Britain, were strongly opposed to this second proposition, and thus while Austria–Hungary increased her territories, Russia got nothing. The Russians were both aggrieved and incensed at this diplomatic defeat, the more so when the German government made it clear in 1909 that if they did not accept it, Germany would support her Austrian ally and impose agreement on Russia by force if necessary. In the aftermath of her defeat at the hands of Japan in the Russo–Japanese war of 1904–5, a militarily weak Russia was forced to accept the situation. But the diplomatic rebuff had the effect of intensifying the determination of Russian leaders to rebuild their country's military strength as quickly as possible and in particular to increase the efficiency and effectiveness of army organisation and mobilisation procedures.

Serbia was even more incensed at the Austrian action than was Russia and stepped up her campaign to appeal to Serbs and Croats beyond her borders to join in a greater Serbia. Secret organizations linked Serbian patriots in Bosnia and Hercegovina with nationalists in the Serbian capital of Belgrade. The Serbs in the Austria–Hungarian Empire also worked closely with other minority groups such as the Czechs. Severe Hungarian repression of Croats and Serbs in Croatia inflamed passions further and encouraged Serb hopes. And Serb appetites were whetted by the Italian military successes in 1911 against the Turkish possessions of Tripolitania and Cyrenaica in North Africa.

Growing Balkans unrest

The Italian victory over Turkish forces in North Africa in late 1911 and subsequent seizure of the Dodecanese Islands in the Aegean in May of the following year, combined with bombardments and naval raids on the Dardanelles, paved the way for a Balkans explosion with possibly catastrophic consequences. The German Kaiser commented in October 1911 that Italy's action might be the first step towards a 'world war with all its terrors'. The Italian Prime Minister, Giolitti, forecast the outcome even before the event, in a remarkably prophetic speech:

> The integrity of what remains of the Ottoman Empire is one of the principles on which the equilibrium and peace of Europe is based. . . . Can it be in the interests of Italy to shatter one of the cornerstones of the old edifice? And what if, after we have attacked Turkey, the Balkans begin to stir? And what if a Balkan war provokes a clash between the two power blocs and a European war? Can it be that we can shoulder the responsibility of putting a match to that powder?

The Balkans did indeed begin to stir with a vengeance after 1911. With the help of the Russian Ambassador in Bulgaria, Serbia and Bulgaria concluded a treaty in March 1912 aimed at driving the Turks out of Europe. Together with Greece and Montenegro, they formed a Balkan League which in October 1912 declared war on Turkey. By the end of November, contrary to the expectations of the German and Austro-Hungarian governments, the League had routed the Turkish armies and driven them out of Europe, apart from Constantinople, the Gallipoli peninsula and some scattered fortresses.

This victory was disastrous for Austria-Hungary. Her enemy Serbia had most ably demonstrated her military prowess, had raised an army some 200,000 strong and was now pressing for an outlet to the Adriatic. Had Russia been prepared to support Serbian claims, it is possible that a general European war might have broken out in late 1912. Austria-Hungary was grimly determined to thwart Serbia's maritime ambitions and would have appealed most strenuously for German assistance. The Russians did indeed make some preliminary military moves, but the Serbs did not pursue their claims, and the Russians did not therefore proceed to any formal measures of mobilization. But in Vienna, in Berlin, in St Petersburg and in Paris the

21

prospect of a European war arising out of Balkan conflicts had been faced as a distinct possibility. It was in December 1912 that the Kaiser and his advisers reviewed their military and naval position and in 1913 that the European arms race really hotted up. The Balkan situation was a major factor in this ominous European lurch towards general war.

The Balkan crisis continued as the Balkan League powers quarrelled amongst themselves during protracted peace negotiations with Turkey. In 1913 Bulgaria attacked her erstwhile allies and was heavily defeated by them. Serbia's influence and territory were further expanded, despite desperate Austrian attempts to contain it by the establishment of the new state of Albania. By the beginning of 1914 the Austro-Hungarian government had been driven to the conclusion that a military confrontation leading to the crushing of Serbia by Austrian troops was absolutely necessary if the Habsburg Empire was to survive. Serbian ambitions, if not destroyed as soon as possible, were bound to lead to the disintegration of the Habsburg Empire as a result of the increasing intensity of Southern Slav campaigns for self determination. Hungarian intransigence and the ambitions of other national groups within the empire seemed to block a peaceful constitutional solution to the problem. Preventive military action against Serbia was seen as the only answer. As the Austrian Chief of Staff, von Hotzendorf, spelled out the choice to Franz Ferdinand,

> The unification of the South Slav race is one of the powerful national movements which can neither be ignored nor kept down. The question can only be, whether unification will take place within the boundaries of the Monarchy – that is at the expense of Serbia's independence – or under Serbia's leadership at the expense of the Monarchy. The cost to the Monarchy would be the loss of its South Slav provinces and thus of almost its entire coastline. The loss of territory and prestige would relegate the Monarchy to the status of a small power.

The Austrian government was well aware that in any confrontation Serbia would inevitably appeal to Russia and that it would be extremely difficult for the Russians not to be drawn in. There were hopes, however, that German threats of military intervention, as in 1909, would serve to keep Russia on the sidelines. The German government itself was alarmed at the deteriorating political and military position of its ally, whose ability to fight against both Serbia and a much strengthened Russian army simultaneously was coming under question. German leaders pressed on their Austrian counterparts the need to take decisive steps to restore their strength and influence in the wake of the Balkan wars while at the same time the German government tried hard to distance itself from any political or military complications arising from the Balkans situation. The Austrian government, in early 1914, decided to start military manoeuvres in Bosnia with a view to preparing an army which could be used to invade Serbia. It was suggested that the Emperor's nephew Franz Ferdinand, successor to the throne and army inspector of the Imperial troops, should pay a visit to the area, both to display his sympathy for the development of southern Slav aspirations within the framework of the Habsburg Empire, and to see how the preparations were advancing. An announcement was made in March 1914 that as part of an official visit to Bosnia, the Archduke Franz Ferdinand and his wife would drive in state through the Bosnian capital, Sarajevo. The date selected for this ceremony was 28 June, a significant date for the Serbs as it marked the anniversary of the Turkish victory at Kosovo in 1389 which had terminated Serbian independence. Extreme nationalist groups in Bosnia began to discuss how best to exploit the visit in as dramatic a way as possible, and Serbian secret organizations and military contacts provided training for would-be terrorists in revolver-shooting and bomb-throwing.

The visit of the archduke was bound to be viewed as provocative by many local inhabitants, and it would obviously offer ample opportunities for demonstrations and disturbances by pro-Serb groups. Yet the Habsburg authorities in the locality took no special precautions, and security on the day of the visit was lax. Travelling in a motor car through the streets of Sarajevo on 28 June, the royal party survived an early bomb attack. Later in the day, however, as the archduke was driving to visit a member of his entourage who had been hurt in this first incident, the royal chauffeur took a fatal wrong turning. This brought the car face to face with another terrorist, Gavrilo Princip, a Bosnian teenager who was brooding over the failure of the morning's assassination attempt. Seizing an opportunity he thought had passed, Princip opened fire and shot Franz Ferdinand dead.

The outbreak of war – July/August 1914

A showdown between Austria-Hungary and Serbia was now inevitable. Though Princip was Bosnian and therefore an Austro-Hungarian subject, it was strongly suspected that he and other terrorists had been supplied with weapons and training from army officers highly placed in the Serbian administration. The opportunity which had now presented itself for the Austrians to take military action against the Serbs was too good to miss, especially in the light of the actual crime committed. The Austrian government was hopeful that the Russians would be so disgusted by the assassination of a royal archduke that they would be loath to be drawn into any resulting conflict between Austria and Serbia. However, before specific military action could be decided upon, it was crucial to check on the attitude of the German government and on the strength of diplomatic and military support likely to be forthcoming from Berlin. The Austrian government therefore sent an envoy to Berlin shortly after the assassination to outline Austrian proposals for action against Serbia and to seek assurances of German support.

It has been suggested by some historians that the delay which this caused gave time for the crisis to escalate, and that had the Austrians invaded Serbia immediately after 28 June, a general European war might not have resulted. But the fact was that Austrian mobilization, whenever it was ordered, was likely to provoke Russian military countermeasures which would have implications for Germany as well as for Austria-Hungary. The German government therefore held the key to the situation. They could work to localize the conflict and to force restraint on Austria-Hungary and on Russia, or they could promise full support to their Austrian ally and run the risk of a general war.

By the summer of 1914 the German government was fully prepared to take the second course. Both the Kaiser and the German Chancellor, Bethmann Hollweg, promised their support to the Austro-Hungarian envoy in meetings held in Berlin on 5 July and pledged assistance to Austria-Hungary in any measures she might take against Serbia. Both were aware that Austro-Hungarian military action was likely to trigger off Russian mobilization which would then necessitate a rapid German military response against both Russia and France. But they could see no acceptable alternative. The Balkan situation was becoming more and more menacing to

Austria-Hungary, and Russia, Serbia's major ally, was increasing daily in military strength. Now seemed as good a moment as any to cut through the intractable political and diplomatic crises facing the Central Powers by taking decisive military action.

On the very day of the assassination of Franz Ferdinand, the Kaiser had been at Kiel attending the celebrations to mark the completion of the widening of the Kiel Canal to enable it to convey full-sized battleships from the Baltic to the North Sea. If a general war should result from the Austro-Serbian conflict, the German army and navy would be at peak strength against their French and Russian opponents, whose military preparations were not yet fully completed, and there was still just an outside possibility that Britain would not intervene. If Austria-Hungary did not take action against Serbia now, Germany might be dragged into a war at some future date when the balance of military power was less favourable. Austria-Hungary was therefore assured on 5 July of complete German support, even in the eventuality of a war with Russia, and was urged to take action against the Serbs as rapidly as possible.

The Austrian ultimatum

It took the Austrian government longer to persuade their Hungarian ministers of the need for military measures against Serbia. The last thing the Hungarians wanted was an increase in the number of Serbs in the Habsburg Empire as a result of a Serb defeat. It took several days for the Austrian leaders to secure the agreement of their Hungarian colleagues to punitive action against Serbia. There then followed the task of framing an ultimatum to the Serbs which their government would find impossible to accept. This was finally achieved by drawing up a list of ten demands to which the Serbian government would have to agree in their entirety and unconditionally. These included the suppression of anti-Austrian propaganda in Serbia, the dissolution of the Serbian nationalist association *Narodna Odbrana*, or Black Hand, widely believed to be responsible for the plotting of the assassination, the purging of officials and army officers guilty of spreading malicious propaganda against Austria, the tightening up of controls on the Serb/Austro-Hungarian frontiers and the participation of Habsburg officials in a Serbian enquiry into the circumstances surrounding the atrocity. Though the text of the ultimatum was agreed on 19 July it was not actually presented to the

Serbian government until 23 July, nearly four weeks after the assassination had taken place. Part of the reason for the delay was to avoid a strong and concerted Franco-Russian reaction. A long-planned state visit to St Petersburg by the French President Poincaré and Prime Minister Viviani was scheduled to take place between 20 and 23 July and the Austrian government did not want to give their Russian and French antagonists the opportunity to plan together and work out measures of joint support for Serbia.

Not until Poincaré and Viviani were safely embarked on board ship for their return journey to France did the Austrian government present their ultimatum to the Serbs. Having delayed so long they now peremptorily demanded a reply within forty-eight hours. Both the shortness of the time allowed to the Serbs for a reply, and the nature of the demands, provoked criticism from other powers who now began to appreciate fully the serious nature of the crisis. The British foreign secretary, Sir Edward Grey, later described the Austrian ultimatum as 'the most formidable document I had ever seen addressed by one state to another that was independent'.

In response to Serbian appeals for help, the Russian government asked the Austrians to extend the time limit for a Serbian reply. They also asked the British government to try to bring pressure to bear on Austria to draw back. Meanwhile they counselled the Serbian government not to resist Austrian invasion if they felt themselves to be too weak, but to entrust their fate 'to the Powers' and to be moderate in their reply to the Austrians. A Russian Council of Ministers meeting on 24 July agreed that, if necessary, the Russians might have to offer military support to the Serbs; preliminary measures which might lead to partial mobilization were authorized, and the following day, the Russian Imperial Council put in train 'The Period Preparatory to War' in European Russia, which involved taking preliminary measures which would facilitate mobilization if and when authorized by the Tsar.

Meanwhile, throughout Europe, the response of Serbia was awaited. Just before the expiry of the time limit at 6 p.m. on 25 July the Serbian reply was received by the Austrians. The Serbian government were prepared to accede, in veiled terms, to nine of the Austrian demands, but they objected to one – the participation of Habsburg officials in the murder investigation to be held by the Serbian authorities. Whether the Serbs were prepared to run the risk of Austrian attack because of assurances of help they had secured from the Russian government is not definitively established, nor is it clearly known whether or not they might have accepted all the demands had Russia put strong pressure on them to do so. Certainly the Serbs had gone most of the way, if not all, towards meeting the Austrian demands. When the Kaiser was later told the details of the Serbian reply, he declared that the grounds for an Austro-Hungarian invasion had been removed, though he added that in his view the Austro-Hungarians would still need to occupy Belgrade until such time as the Serbs were actually seen to be carrying out their promises.

The Austrian government needed no such encouragement. Since the Serbs had not unconditionally accepted the ultimatum, diplomatic relations with Serbia were immediately severed and on the evening of 25 July, Austria ordered the mobilization of seven army corps against Serbia and a further one as a precaution against Italy. Although the troops would not be in a position to attack Serbia until 12 August at the earliest, the Austrian government was anxious to make a formal declaration of war and to move towards the outbreak of hostilities as soon as possible. They were accordingly very cool towards the efforts of Sir Edward Grey to mediate in the crisis.

Attempts at mediation

Once the gravity of the crisis was appreciated in London, Grey began to try to put pressure on the French, German and Italian governments to co-operate with Britain in a joint approach to the Austrian and Russian governments to refrain from mobilization. But Grey's attempts to convene a traditional-style great power conference to settle the dispute only had the effect of strengthening Austria's resolve to proceed to military measures against Serbia as rapidly as possible. And the German government assisted Austria by informing Grey that in their view the dispute could most effectively be settled by direct negotiations between Austria and Russia. Without German support, Grey's efforts were unlikely to have any significant impact. Grey, however, persisted in his efforts, and tried to induce the Austrian government to accept the Serbian reply to its ultimatum as at least a basis for negotiations. This further attempt did have the effect of causing considerable embarrassment to the Germans. The German Chancellor, Bethmann Hollweg wrote to the Austrian government:

Having already declined the English plan for a Conference, it is impossible for us entirely to reject this suggestion as well. By refusing every mediatory action we should make ourselves responsible before the whole world for the conflagration and should appear as the real authors of war. That would make our position impossible at home where we must appear to have war forced upon us. Our situation is all the more difficult since Serbia has apparently given way a great deal. We cannot therefore decline the role of mediator and must forward the English proposal to the Vienna cabinet for consideration.

By the time this telegram reached Vienna, however, the Austrian government had already decided to make a formal declaration of war on Serbia on the following day, 28 July, and on 29 July, the ships of their Danube flotilla bombarded Belgrade.

The Russian military response

The Russian government had already resolved to respond to an Austrian declaration of war against Serbia by the mobilization of four Russian military districts, Odessa, Kiev, Moscow, and Kazan, which would enable an army to be raised against Austria. There was a strong belief in government and court circles that Serbia could not be left to face Austria-Hungary alone as this would seriously damage the credibility of Russia as a great power and as a protector of Balkan Slavs, particularly in the light of Russia's failure to act in 1909 and 1912. Furthermore, an Austrian victory would increase the strength of the Central European 'German bloc' at the expense of the Slavs and weaken Russia's chances of exploiting Turkish decline in the region of Constantinople. The Russian foreign secretary therefore informed the Russian ambassadors in Berlin, Vienna, Paris, London and Rome on 28 July that it was planned to start the mobilization of Russian troops and of the Baltic and Black Sea fleets the next day. The hope was that Austria-Hungary might be induced to negotiate a compromise settlement with Serbia at the news of such decisive Russian action. If she refused, Russia would be ready to assist Serbia.

But the Russian General Staff now became alarmed that such partial mobilization against Austria-Hungary might hamper the effectiveness of a general mobilization should this become necessary. They were naturally concerned that Germany might respond to

Russian partial mobilization by a full mobilization of its own which would take effect much more speedily than the Russian one. While the Russians were switching from partial to general mobilization, their north-west borders would be open to German attack. The Russian military authorities now pressed for general mobilization and were strongly supported by French diplomatic pressure. France was concerned that, if attacked by Germany, the Russians should raise an army as speedily as they could to invade East Prussia. The French government was well aware that it would take the Russians three or four weeks to mobilize fully, and therefore tried to pressurize the Russian government to authorize general mobilization as quickly as possible.

The Russian leadership now hesitated between partial and general mobilization measures. Fearful of the consequences of any decision he might make, the Russian Tsar sent a telegram to his cousin the Kaiser on 29 July, appealing for his help in avoiding the outbreak of war, and warning: 'I foresee that very soon I shall be overwhelmed by the pressure brought upon me and be forced to take extreme measures which will lead to war'. The news which now arrived of the Austrian bombardment of Belgrade hardened the resolve of Russian ministers and the Chief of the General Staff. They decided, in the words of the foreign secretary,

> that in view of the small probability of avoiding a war with Germany it was indispensable to prepare for it in every way in good time, and that therefore the risk could not be accepted of delaying a general mobilization later by effecting a partial mobilization now. The conclusion reached at this conference was at once reported by telephone to the Tsar who authorised the taking of steps accordingly.

However, just as the general mobilization order was about to be despatched throughout Russia, an instruction to substitute partial mobilization was received from the Tsar: he had just received a friendly reply to his telegram from Kaiser William II and still had hopes of averting war with Germany by ordering only partial mobilization aimed at Austria.

Even partial mobilization by Russia, however, was sufficient to cause considerable concern to the German military authorities, if not to the Kaiser. They were alarmed at the prospect of Austria committing the bulk of her troops to an invasion of Serbia, while leaving only small defence forces behind to cope with a Russian onslaught. German military planning had assumed that in a situation of general war between the Central Powers and their opponents, the Austrians would cover the German military offensive against France by launching a great offensive against Russia in Poland. If Austrian troops were instead fully committed in the Balkans, the German eastern borders would be left vulnerable to Russian attack, thus endangering the success of the Schlieffen plan. While the German Chancellor was by the end of July becoming worried about the escalating situation, and trying to put the brakes on Austrian preparations for war, the German Chief of Staff von Moltke was urging the Austrians to announce general mobilization against Russia, and was promising unqualified German support in a European war. The Austrian government, resolved to act, needed little prompting.

The Russian authorities were by now desperately worried that partial mobilization would weaken their ability to meet a German attack. Rumours were circulating in St Petersburg that the Austrians were about to declare general mobilization and that the Germans were also taking preliminary mobilization measures. Strong pressure from their French allies to take action under the terms of the alliance by invading East Prussia as quickly as possible reinforced their own resolve to get the Tsar to revert back to the order for general mobilization. On the afternoon of 30 July, the Tsar was finally prevailed upon to proclaim the order for general mobilization, and the following day the Austrian emperor followed suit. Clearly a general European war was now inevitable and the German military machine was primed for action. Germany demanded that Russia cease all military activities aimed against Austria and Germany within twelve hours. In the absence of a reply, Germany declared war on Russia on 1 August and began to mobilize her troops. But the immediate German attack fell not on Russia but on Belgium and France. On 2 August the German government presented an ultimatum to the Belgian government, demanding a passage for German armies through neutral Belgium, which the Belgians indignantly rejected. The French government, fully aware of the threat facing them, had already ordered mobilization on 1 August, and two days later Germany declared war on France, on trumped-up charges of French frontier violations and an alleged bombing attack on Nuremberg. On 4 August, German troops crossed the Belgian frontier.

Britain enters the fray

This unprovoked German invasion of a European neighbour whose neutrality had been guaranteed by all the European great powers since 1839 was bound to draw the British government into the conflict because of the strategic threat posed as much as the violation of international law. Up to this point, the British government's reactions to the crisis unfolding in Europe had been muted despite the *entente* with France and Russia. Sir Edward Grey had attempted to convene a great power conference to settle the crisis, and when this had not proved acceptable to Germany, he had attempted to mediate directly between Austria and Russia and had failed. But he would not at this stage be drawn on what measures the British government might take in a war involving the continental powers, and in what circumstances Britain might intervene on the side of France and Russia. It has been suggested by L. C. F. Turner that a firm British announcement 'that Britain would be sure to intervene on the side of France might have deterred Bethmann Hollweg from pushing Austria into her suicidal declaration of war on Serbia, but no specific warning was forthcoming from Grey until 29 July'. Grey himself was concerned that such a positive British pledge might provoke the Russians and the French into action, and as we have seen he did not abandon hopes of trying to settle the conflict through diplomatic means until very late in July. There would have been little point in trying to bring pressure on the Russian government to resolve the crisis in talks with the Austrians, if at the same time Grey was pledging British military support. Besides, he could not be certain at this stage of full cabinet backing for such a positive British declaration of intent.

The German government certainly hoped that Britain would remain neutral in the event of the outbreak of a European war and some of its diplomatic activities were influenced by this consideration. On the other hand, the German military authorities were not particularly worried about the immediate military effect of British intervention, even in the shape of a British Expeditionary Force some 150,000 strong. This had been taken into account in their military planning and merely reinforced the importance of an immediate invasion of Belgium and speedy capture of Liège in the event of a general war so that the fighting in the west would be over before the British forces could become involved. Under no circumstances would the British government be willing to stand aside and watch the

German armies overrun Belgium in an unprovoked attack, and the German civilian leaders were deluding themselves if they thought that they could both operate the Schlieffen plan and anticipate British neutrality. The British cabinet had little hesitation at its meeting of 3 August in deciding to respond to the German invasion of Belgium by an ultimatum requesting the withdrawal of German troops. When this was disregarded Britain declared war on Germany on 4 August, and authorized the despatch of the British Expeditionary Force two days later. Only Italy, of Europe's great powers, managed to stay on the sidelines by declaring that, because of Austria's aggression against Serbia, the terms of the Triple Alliance did not apply. The other five major powers were at war, just over six weeks after the assassination of Franz Ferdinand. In the celebrated words of Sir Edward Grey, 'The lamps are going out all over Europe. We shall not see them lit again in our lifetime'.

2
The historical debate

The European war which broke out in August 1914 was expected to be a short one. The German Crown prince looked forward to a 'bright and jolly war'. No European government had made extensive economic or military plans for a prolonged struggle – the Russian Ministry of War in 1914 was typical, in preparing for a struggle of two to six months. Belief in the power of the offensive to deliver a rapid knockout blow to the enemy was strong, though developments in military technology since 1871 should have suggested otherwise. Furthermore, it was assumed that the economic consequences of a lengthy conflict would be so ruinous that European countries would be brought to their knees by financial chaos within months. Sir Edward Grey, in July 1914, had speculated that a European war involving Austria, France, Russia and Germany 'must involve the expenditure of so vast a sum of money and such interference with trade, that a war would be accompanied or followed by a complete collapse of European credit and industry'. In declaring war against each other in 1914 the European great powers envisaged a series of short, sharp, military encounters, to be followed presumably by a general conference of the belligerents, which would confirm the military results by a political and diplomatic settlement. The confident British expectation that its expeditionary forces would be home by Christmas was echoed in the other capitals of Europe.

In the event, the war lasted four-and-a-quarter years, and though it certainly had the grievous financial consequences prophesied by Grey, it is mainly remembered for its huge toll of suffering and human life. The Austro-Hungarian and Russian Empires fell apart before the war's end, and the Turkish Empire crumbled soon after. Britain and France could only drive back the German armies in France and Belgium with the help of the United States of America which entered the war in 1917. Not surprisingly the debate after 1918 about the responsibility for causing the war was strongly coloured by its heavy cost and enormously far-reaching consequences which were certainly not foreseen in 1914. The war which actually occurred was not the war for which the European governments before 1914 had been preparing. This important consideration has to be borne in mind when discussing the question of responsibility for the events of July and early August 1914.

The verdict of Versailles

In order to justify the levying of heavy war reparations on the German government, the Versailles peace treaty of 1919 stated unequivocally in Article 231 that

> The Allied and Associated Governments affirm and Germany accepts the responsibility of Germany and her allies for causing all the loss and damage to which the Allied and Associated Governments and their nationals have been subjected as a consequence of the war imposed upon them by the aggression of Germany and her allies.

The treaty also singled out the German Kaiser for blame 'for the supreme offence against international morality and the sanctity of treaties'. There were attempts to bring the Kaiser to trial from his refuge in Holland, but these were unsuccessful since the Dutch authorities refused to hand him over to the allied powers. While delegates of the new Weimar republican government in Germany signed the treaty of Versailles under protest, there was little willingness in Germany to accept sole responsibility for causing the war. Article 231 was attacked as a politically motivated slight on the part of vengeful enemies against a country which was no more guilty than any other of plotting to start a war in 1914.

The German response

The German interpretation of the situation which had faced their country before 1914 was of a Germany increasingly encircled by an aggressive alignment of Russia, France and Britain. She had had no alternative but to try to break out. This was widely believed, not just in 1914 or in 1918, but throughout the inter-war period. A popular German textbook of the 1920s, in use in secondary schools throughout the country, explained the situation as follows:

> In the so-called peace treaty, the unheard of demand for reparations and the unexampled exploitation of Germany was founded on the lie regarding Germany's war guilt. Did Germany desire the war, did she prepare it maliciously and begin it wantonly? Today every informed person inside and outside Germany knows that Germany is absolutely innocent with regard to the outbreak of war. Russia, France and England wanted war and unleashed it.

Weimar Germany never accepted the findings of Article 231, and leaders of successive governments believed that if they could show that the detested 'war guilt' clause was a lie, then the ethical basis for the payment of reparations would disappear and the way would be open for wholesale revision of the entire treaty. A special branch of the German Foreign Office was set up, the War Guilt Section, which organized, financed and directed two main units. One was a Working Committee of German Associations for Combating Lies Concerning War Responsibility, which circulated literature to trade unions, clubs and employers' associations. The other was a Centre for the Study of the Causes of War, a more intellectually orientated operation, which recruited scholars, journalists and teachers to demonstrate the inaccuracy of Article 231 and, by extension, the whole treaty. Forty volumes of material were published between 1922 and 1927, based mainly on German Foreign Office archives and, significantly, excluding material from General Staff records, Navy Office files or the Ministry of War. Some documents have since been found to have been falsified, and crucial episodes were completely ignored, such as the Potsdam meetings between the Austrian envoy, the Kaiser and Chancellor Bethmann-Hollweg on 5–6 July, 1914, at which the German 'blank cheque' was issued to the Austrian government.

German interpretations of events in 1914 centred on the aggression of the Serbian government, which allegedly had very close links with the Black Hand assassins. Austria had to meet this challenge, and Germany had no option but to support her ally. Britain should have helped Germany to localize the conflict, but in any event this would have been virtually impossible because of full Russian mobilization in support of Serbia, and Russia's aggressive designs in the Balkan and Black Sea region. The German conclusion was that no single nation was responsible for the events of 1914, and certainly not Germany. Some German historians acknowledged that there might have been miscalculations on the part of German leaders, such as the Kaiser's belief that, because a royal heir to the throne had been murdered, Tsar Nicholas II would not support Serbia and condone such an act, or a mistaken perception that Britain might stay neutral in the face of an unfolding war on the European mainland, but these errors of judgement did not in any way lead to unwarranted German aggression.

Diplomatic interpretations

Germany's massive output of documents and publications in the 1920s provoked other governments into publishing their prewar diplomatic records to show that they, too, had nothing to hide. Eleven volumes of British *Documents on the Origins of the War* appeared between 1926 and 1938, along with eight Austrian volumes and a number of French ones. Russian diplomats in exile after 1917 published extracts from their embassy archives and official Italian government documents appeared after the Second World War. No Serbian documents, however, were published until 1980.

By the 1930s, therefore, the diplomatic dealings between the European governments in the years, months, weeks and days before August 1914 were known about in immense detail. They provoked allegations that the war had been brought about by a complex web of secret diplomatic dealings, by the existence in Europe of an increasingly rigid 'alliance system' and by the machinations of ambassadors and army officers. A book published in 1926 by a Cambridge academic, G. Lowes Dickinson, entitled *The International Anarchy*, portrayed the total bankruptcy of the old European diplomatic system, while its author hailed the new era of collective diplomacy which would ensure peace under the watchful eye of the League of Nations. This view of a general European breakdown before 1914 was shared by two very different world leaders after 1918, the United States

President, Woodrow Wilson, and the leader of the new Bolshevik regime, Lenin.

Woodrow Wilson believed very strongly that secret diplomacy and the selfish greed of the pre-war European great powers had brought them into collision in 1914. Only a transformation of the way in which the international system operated would prevent wars from breaking out in the future, and hence he saw his great mission as the establishment of a League of Nations. At the Paris Peace Conference, he had insisted on incorporating the text of the Covenant of the League of Nations into each of the peace treaties. Many League enthusiasts in Britain in the inter-war period shared Wilson's distrust of pre-war secret diplomacy, and his view of a general European diplomatic breakdown in 1914. So did two American academics, Harry Barnes and Sidney Fay. In 1925, Barnes, a Professor of Historical Sociology, wrote a book called *The Genesis of World War*, largely to express his anger at war in general, and at the authors of the Great War in particular, whom he deemed to be the Serbian and Russian governments. Three years later, Fay, a colleague of his at Smith University, produced a two-volume *Origins of the World War*. He exonerated the Serbian government and believed Germany should not have promised her Austrian ally a free hand against Serbia, but he blamed this on the Kaiser's short-sighted diplomacy, and not on a general German attitude of aggression. Fay's conclusion was that it was Russian mobilization which precipitated the final catastrophe leading to German mobilization, but that it was the reckless policy of Austria-Hungary which made her more responsible than any other power for the immediate origin of the war. As for Germany, she never planned for war in 1914 and did not want it.

Fay's assessment was extremely influential both in the United States and in Britain for the next thirty years, though it was immediately challenged by Renouvin in France and by Schmitt in the United States. Both these historians placed their emphasis on the dangerous gamble which Germany took in 1914 by giving full support to Austria and counting on the willingness of Russia to accept diplomatic defeat. Schmitt argued that the two Central Powers were out to alter the balance of power in the Balkans and that this was bound to provoke Russia into a military response. Therefore German policy was belligerent and dangerously aggressive.

An imperialist war?

A very different perspective on the pre-war European situation was put forward by Lenin in 1916 in his pamphlet *Imperialism – The Highest Stage of Capitalism*. He portrayed the Great War as an imperialist war, caused by rivalries triggered off by the pressures of highly organized financial monopolies operating in the different European countries. Lenin argued that capitalism had reached its highest stage in the form of imperialism and that frenzied competition amongst commercial rivals for markets and for raw materials had inevitably brought about war. On taking power in Russia in late 1917, one of the first actions of the new Bolshevik regime was to publish secret documents which they found in the Tsarist archives. The contents of these confidential memoranda and diplomatic agreements revealed the spoils of war and the imperialist booty in the form of Constantinople and other Turkish possessions that the Russian government had been promised by the British and French governments as a result of victories to be won against Germany, Austria-Hungary and Turkey. The Bolshevik government denounced such agreements and proceeded to renounce all imperialist gains and concessions accruing to the Tsarist government since the late nineteenth century.

In the 1920s and 1930s, communists and socialists throughout Europe produced many critiques emphasizing the close and, they argued, inevitable connections between capitalism and war, and the important role imperialism had played in arousing tensions and driving nations to war in 1914. This line of analysis is still to be found in more recent accounts of the origins of the First World War and was accepted as the orthodox Marxist 'explanation' of the outbreak of war in 1914 in eastern European communist regimes after 1945. As late as 1968, East German historians were arguing that the First World War constituted 'a quarrel among the imperialists for a new division of the world'. Monopoly capitalists and *Junker* agrarians, assisted by the military, unleashed the war which was inevitable owing to the 'conflicts inherent to the capitalist social order'.

However, there are several important aspects of such lines of argument which have been vigorously disputed by non-Marxist historians. The view that states with a capitalist mode of production are bound to become involved in wars because of internally generated conflicts and clashes with other powers over access to raw materials and territories is a very general proposition which does not fit very closely the particular circumstances of 1914. For a start, there was no shortage of wars in precapitalist eras, and in the nineteenth century there were many wars throughout the world involving non-capitalist states. Neither Serbia nor Austria-Hungary could possibly be regarded as highly-developed capitalist states of the sort Lenin wrote about, and there is little evidence that highly organized financial monopolies and trading interests pressurized the Russian or French governments into pursuing the policies they actually followed in 1914. Furthermore, many economic and colonial issues which had been causing friction between French, German and British governments before 1914, such as the financing of the Berlin–Baghdad railway and the future disposition of the Portuguese colonies, had been resolved by the summer of 1914. Because of a very narrow, largely economic definition of the word 'imperialism', socialist and Marxist accounts of the origins of the First World War have laid emphasis on colonial clashes and on economic rivalries which other historians have regarded as of secondary importance.

Certainly new 'economic' imperialism of the sort referred to by Lenin can be discerned in some of the policies pursued by the British, French and German companies and trading interests in Africa and the Far East from the 1880s onwards, and they did generate considerable economic and political tensions which their home governments often found difficult to resolve. But such colonial and trading disputes, while they may have contributed to a more inflamed international atmosphere, were largely resolved by the end of the first decade of the twentieth century. Far more of a threat to international stability was posed by the older and more traditional imperial rivalries, involving struggles for power in areas regarded as strategically and militarily important. These rivalries provoked the most serious clashes: Austria-Hungary's attempt to impose its will on Serbia, Russia's hopes to spread its influence in the Near East, the dreams of the pan-German nationalists to secure German mastery of the Russian steppes. It was not the capitalist system as such which was giving rise to ambition, but traditional desires for prestige and influence and great power status. These may well have been sharpened directly or indirectly by economic competition and by the development of industry, but they were not caused primarily by these factors.

Some critics in the inter-war period blamed individual capitalists, and particularly armaments manufacturers, for the spiralling arms race in Europe before 1914 and for the consequent outbreak of war, citing as evidence the growing economic and naval rivalry between Britain and Germany. In fact, most European banks and businesses stood to lose rather than to gain from war in 1914. Britain was Germany's best customer in that year, while Russia sent 44 per cent of her exports to Germany and took 47 per cent of imports from her. It was widely assumed that war would bring about the collapse of economic stability and civilized life and that all owners of property and of capital would be the losers. There is no evidence that great industrialists and weapons manufacturers were egging their governments on to war in 1914; on the contrary, they were fearful of the consequences of a conflagration.

An accidental slide into war?

However, the essential point which was common to both the American and Marxist interpretations of 1914 which appeared in the inter-war period was that no single nation or alliance could be held responsible for the outbreak of war. If guilt was appropriate, it should be shared. If the breakdown of the entire European diplomatic system or the development of an advanced stage of capitalism was to blame, this was beyond the control of a single nation. By the late 1930s, the view which prevailed most strongly about the origins of the war was the one put forward by David Lloyd George, British Prime Minister from 1916 to 1922, in his *War Memoirs*, that 'the nations in 1914 slithered over the brink into the boiling cauldron of war'. There was no general 'will to war'; the crisis escalated, nations were carried away despite themselves and a war broke out which no single country really wanted.

More recent historical work has suggested a variant on this theme. L. C. F. Turner, in his *Origins of the First World War* (1967), drew attention to the miscalculations made by leading statesmen in the various European countries, especially in Germany, and to the failure of the civilian leaders throughout Europe to appreciate until too late the military implications of their decisions. Other historians have drawn attention to the predominance of military decision-making in 1914 and to the eclipse of the power and influence of civilian leaders by high-ranking and power-hungry military and naval leaders throughout the great European capitals. In Germany, the distinguished historian Gerhard Ritter devoted much of his academic life to an exhaustive and critical examination of the problem of militarism in Germany, which resulted ultimately in a four-volume publication which appeared in English in the early 1970s as *The Sword and the Sceptre*. While he found much to criticize in the growing power and ascendancy of the military elites in Wilhelmine Germany, he none the less still believed, in 1960, that German political and military leaders had been overwhelmed by the crisis of 1914 and that 'we have no right to doubt the genuineness of their basic desire for peace. No one in a position of authority wanted to bring about a world war'.

But this line of analysis, which seeks to suggest that the outbreak of war in 1914 was really an accident arising out of a crisis in which events careered out of control, is not supported by the full weight of historical evidence now available. There was no equivocation on the part of Austria-Hungary after 28 June, as Samuel Williamson's study, *Austria-Hungary and the Origins of the First World War* (1991), clearly demonstrates. She was determined to exact military revenge on Serbia. Equally, the Russian government was not prepared to capitulate to Austrian demands or German ultimata as she had in 1909, but was resolved to support Serbia if she was attacked. As authoritative recent studies by David Stevenson, *Armaments and the Coming of War* (1996) and by David Herrman, *The Arming of Europe and the Making of the First World War* (1996) have shown, the German government was well aware that Russia might be drawn in the Austro-Serbian conflict but nonetheless gave full support to her Austrian ally and prepared herself for any military consequences which might arise. The French government was concerned to honour the terms of her alliance with Russia even if this meant war, rather than taking the risk of seeing Russia destroyed or of losing her support in a future crisis. And even British leaders were convinced of the need to preserve the balance of military power on the European mainland. Certainly there came a point, in late July, when military considerations took precedence over diplomatic ones, but these stemmed from political decisions which had been taken by the various governments concerned in the previous four weeks, and from perceptions and fears which had been taking shape for many months if not years.

Austria-Hungary and the nationalities problem

Some studies of the origins of the war have focused on the intractable nationality issues causing so much conflict in eastern Europe in the late nineteenth and early twentieth centuries. In his Historical Association pamphlet, *The Origins of the First World War* (1958), Bernadotte Schmitt argued that the primary cause of war in 1914 was the denial of self-determination to minority groups. 'More than any other circumstance', he maintained, 'this conflict between existing governments and their unhappy minorities was responsible for the catastrophe of 1914.' The tension which arose throughout eastern Europe as a result of political frontiers cutting across lines of nationality was especially acute in the Habsburg Empire and gave rise to the bitter conflict between Austria-Hungary and Serbia.

There has been much debate amongst historians about the foreign policy pursued by the Habsburg rulers and the extent to which it was motivated by defensive or aggressive considerations and by internal or external factors. Many historians have portrayed Austria's external policy in the years before 1914 as primarily defensive, aimed at keeping the peace in the Balkans and working to prevent any change in the balance of power there. They argue that this strategy of containment was fatally undermined by the sudden collapse of Turkish power in Europe in 1912, and that after this date Austria faced the prospect of a desperate struggle for her own survival as a great power. F. R. Bridge, in *The Coming of the First World War* (1983), argued that both Austria-Hungary and Russia were motivated in their Balkan policies by a quest for security which brought them into constant conflict. However, the existence of the Turkish Empire in south-east Europe acted as a stabilizing factor, operating as a 'shock absorber in the international system'. It was only when this buffer between the great powers was suddenly removed, after the Balkan Wars of 1912–13, that serious conflict in the Balkans became inevitable and a peaceful solution to Austria's problems proved impossible to achieve.

However, some historians have depicted Austria's attempts to crush Serbia as aggressive and totally reckless. Unwilling or unable to solve internal problems, her government has been criticized for embarking on a suicidal mission against Serbia which was bound to involve her in war with Russia, and possibly other powers as well. It has been pointed out that, on no fewer than twenty-five occasions between 1913 and 1914, the Austrian Chief of Staff, Conrad von

Hotzendorf, urged war against Serbia. Yet it must also be emphasized that Emperor Franz Joseph himself was opposed to a military confrontation and believed that the competing national and racial aspirations within the Habsburg Empire could best be kept within reasonable bounds by international peace. His heir, Franz Ferdinand, whose assassination triggered off Austrian military action against Serbia, was known to be sympathetic to southern Slav ambitions and to be trying to shape a new 'trialist' structure within the Austro-Hungarian Empire which would replace German-Magyar domination by a German-Magyar-Slav combination. Many historians have denied that the external policy pursued by the Austrian government between 1912 and 1914 was unduly influenced by domestic considerations. Much more significant in influencing Austrian policy, they argue, was the German government's reluctance to support Austrian interests during the Balkan Wars or to recognize the growing danger posed by Serbia. Because the German government sought to distance itself from the Balkan crisis, the Austrian government felt itself to be increasingly isolated in the face of a mounting challenge from Serbia, behind which lurked the prospect of a Balkan Federation linked to Russia. It was this external threat, it is argued, rather than domestic considerations, which motivated Austria's policy in the Balkans in 1914 and caused it to become more and more desperate.

However, there is general agreement that German decision-making was a crucial element in the tense situation after the June assassination. Without the assurance of German support, given so instantly and unequivocally to Austria on 5 July by the Kaiser and German Chancellor, Austria would not have embarked on her fatal confrontation with Serbia. It has been widely asserted that German policy held the key to the situation in the summer of 1914 and that it was the German desire to profit diplomatically and militarily from the crisis which widened the conflict from an eastern European one to a continental and world war.

The case for 'German responsibility'

The outbreak of the Second World War brought to the fore renewed accusations of German responsibility for causing the First World War as well. Events in the late 1930s and German ambitions as revealed in the course of the Second World War seemed to demonstrate a continuity in German foreign policy which was aimed since 1871 at European and possibly world domination. In his book *The Struggle For Mastery in Europe, 1848–1918* (1954), A. J. P. Taylor presented a picture of German rulers bidding aggressively for continental supremacy before 1914 and frightening Britain, France and Russia into a defensive alignment in a desperate bid to contain German political and economic power. Whereas other historians had laid great emphasis on Russian general mobilization for causing an escalation of the crisis, Taylor emphasized the importance of German military planning which her neighbours were forced to take account of and respond to accordingly. Taylor also argued that it was not the existence of the balance of power system which led to war in 1914 but its breakdown, vigorously assisted by German policy aims since the late nineteenth century.

Similar conclusions had been reached in the previous decade by an Italian journalist, Luigi Albertini, whose three-volume study of the outbreak of the war, *The Origins of the War of 1914*, was published between 1942 and 1943 but did not reach an English audience until the 1950s. Albertini had gone through all the available documents and interviewed all surviving participants; his exhaustive analysis of the crisis led him to the conclusion that German support for Austria in early July 1914 constituted a very risky gamble and that German mobilization was equivalent to war, because of the Schlieffen plan. Though he acknowledged the fact that Russian policy escalated the crisis, that the Serbs had no intention of compromising with Austria and that Grey could have warned the Germans earlier of likely British intervention, he concluded that 'final, definite responsibility for the outbreak of the war lies with the German plan of mobilisation'.

These renewed attempts to look critically at German diplomatic and military policies before 1914 were still being countered in the 1950s by the 'revisionist' view, expressed by a committee of distinguished French and German historians in 1952, that 'the documents do not permit attributing to any government or nation a premeditated desire for European war in 1914'. However, by the early 1960s, documents began to be produced from the Imperial German archives in Potsdam which were to challenge this assertion in the strongest possible terms.

The 'Fischer Thesis'

In 1961, a Professor of History at Hamburg University, Fritz Fischer, brought out a book entitled *Griff nach der Weltmacht*, which was published in England in 1966 under the rather different title, *Germany's Aims in the First World War*. Fischer's lengthy and detailed work, based on extensive and meticulous archival research, sought to expose the extent of German annexationist aims in the First World War and to suggest that the German government provoked war in order to achieve them. Not surprisingly, the book caused an immediate sensation and provoked a great outcry amongst fellow historians which centred particularly on three of Fischer's assertions. The first was that the German government accepted, and indeed hoped, that a major European war would result from its backing of Serbia against Austria. The second, especially provocative in the immediate aftermath of the Second World War, was that the annexationist war aims of the Imperial government not only predated the outbreak of war but also showed a remarkable similarity to the plans made by the Nazis for conquest after 1933. The third contentious point was Fischer's assertion that the sources of German expansionism were to be found less in Germany's international position than in her social, economic and political domestic situation on the eve of war.

In coming to such conclusions, Fischer had had the benefit of access to the Imperial archives in Potsdam, since 1945 located in East Germany. This in itself annoyed the West German historical establishment, but it was the use to which he put his documentary findings – to frame a charge of general German responsibility for the outbreak of war in 1914 – which really enraged his critics. He did not share Gerhard Ritter's belief that civilian leaders, such as the Chancellor, Bethmann-Hollweg, had been misled or dominated by the military. Indeed, he argued that the sources revealed no substantial difference in approach or in objectives between the civilian and military decision-makers.

For the next few years, Fischer's work was the subject of great controversy, and he himself was subjected to bitter personal attack. The West German government cancelled funding for a lecture tour Fischer had arranged to undertake in the United States. But the staunchness with which Fischer defended his views, and the documentary material which became available during the 1960s, much of it collected by Fischer's former pupil Imanuel Geiss, forced Fischer's critics to look again at the policies pursued by German leaders in 1914. They began to admit, grudgingly, that German strategy in 1914 had been a high-risk one, but argued that it had been justified by the growing Russian military build-up and construction of railways in her western provinces. Pessimism about the future, and in particular about the inexorable growth of Russian power, grew amongst both civilian and military leaders in Germany in 1914, it was argued, and made them willing to run the risk of war: not to achieve aggressive objectives but to secure Germany's position as a great power.

This view was strongly challenged by Fischer in a second major work which came out in 1969 and appeared in English in 1975 under the title *War of Illusions*. The focus of this book was on German policy between 1911 and 1914, and Fischer drew on detailed documentary evidence to substantiate his charge that there was a strong 'will to war' amongst German leaders before 1914, and to refute the notion that German ruling circles in 1914 had acted only to protect their interests in the face of a growing threat of encirclement from the three *entente* powers. In particular, he drew attention to the personal diary of Admiral Müller, which had been published in 1965 and which referred to a meeting between the Kaiser and his chief military and naval advisers on 8 December 1912. The Kaiser had been informed by his new Ambassador in London that, in the event of a German attack on France, Britain would come to France's aid. This revelation sparked off a general review of the European situation in the course of which the Chief of the General Staff, von Moltke, commented, 'In my opinion war is inevitable, and the sooner the better.' This view appeared to be generally endorsed by those present at the meeting. It was also agreed that the public should be 'better prepared' through the press for war against Russia. Fischer laid great emphasis on this 'war council' meeting, and argued that it revealed a clear intention on the part of Germany's leaders to wage a European war at the earliest favourable opportunity.

Fischer's researches also laid great emphasis on the social and political structure of Wilhelmine Germany and on the power wielded by a set of autocratic, militaristic *Junkers* who were violently anti-democratic and anti-modern. They felt their domestic position to be under threat from the forces of social democracy and their world aspirations to be increasingly blocked by the 'encirclement' policies of France, Russia and Britain and by their own lack of investment capital. Fischer's claim that it was domestic, social and political factors which were instrumental in shaping Germany's increasingly aggressive foreign policy after 1911 was taken up and developed in detail in the 1970s by a younger generation of German historians.

The primacy of domestic policy

Traditional German historical scholarship, based on the writings of the great nineteenth-century historian Ranke, had emphasized the *Primat der Aussenpolitik* (primacy of foreign policy), arguing that external considerations dictated the course of German foreign policy from 1870 and that internal policies were of necessity tailored to meet the requirements of the international situation. In the 1970s, this belief was turned on its head, and many historians put forward the argument that it was the *Primat der Innenpolitik* (primacy of domestic policy) which was crucial in shaping Germany's foreign policy decisions before 1914. A generation of younger German historians portrayed Wilhelmine Germany as dominated by a pre-industrial elite, mainly of Prussian *Junkers*, whose values and beliefs derived from an earlier age. They were bitterly resistant to new ideas and economic developments, which they regarded as immensely threatening to their political pre-eminence and power, and they clung ever more tenaciously to their social position and political privileges. The seemingly irresistible march of democratic forces and the rise of bourgeois and proletarian power threatened their entire existence and way of life, and this domestic challenge became linked in their minds with the external encirclement Germany was facing and the challenge of bourgeois Britain and republican France. Historians have pointed out that many aristocrats in Germany after 1910 were deeply pessimistic about the future and saw their situation in stark terms of black and white choices; either they clung on grimly to power and took whatever measures were necessary to ensure their dominance in the face of greater and greater challenges or they made concessions and faced the prospect of irreversible decline. It was necessary to stand firm both at home and abroad; world power would strengthen their power domestically, but the decline of German power abroad would lead to social and economic eclipse at home.

Fischer argued that it was ultimately the determination of the German power elite to resist all social, political and constitutional changes within the *Reich* which led to the adoption of a 'forward erratic and aggressive policy'. Hans-Ulrich Wehler argued that social

47

imperialism in Germany was 'the diversion outwards of internal tensions and forces of change in order to preserve the social and political status quo' and that it was a 'defensive ideology' aimed against 'the disruptive effects of industrialisation on the social and economic structure of Germany'. In *The German Empire 1871–1918* (1973, published in English in 1985) Wehler concluded that 'it was not the alignment of forces outside its borders which imposed a certain course of action on Germany but . . . this was primarily a product of the decisions arising from its internal political situation'.

German fears of encirclement

However Berghahn, in *Germany and the Approach of War in 1914* (1973), while accepting the importance of domestic factors in shaping German foreign policy, argued that they should be considered alongside external factors, as the two sets of considerations were interdependent. He drew attention to the gap which appeared to exist in Germany between reality and the 'warped perception of it which resulted time and again in serious miscalculations'. German decision-makers, whether viewing internal problems or external ones, saw them in a seriously distorted form which gravely affected the rationality of their policies. Herwig in *Knowing One's Enemies* (May (ed.) 1984) developed this theme further. He drew attention to the perceptional framework of the German leadership which conditioned their thinking:

> From being cock of the walk with seemingly not unreasonable ambitions for global expansion, imperial Germany had been reduced to a condition where it could not even work its will upon the Turks. The navy had turned out to be an engine of weakness rather than of strength. The Empire's only sure ally was the Hapsburg domain, which the Wilhemstrasse accurately characterised as the new 'sick man of Europe'.

Added to this were the 'disquieting electoral trends symbolised by the Social-Democratic electoral victories' and 'by the fact that the army's expansion would have to be financed by taxes on inherited wealth and that the army's officer corps, like the navy's, came increasingly from outside the old aristocracy'. Herwig portrayed the German ruling elite as 'ridden with anxiety, guilt, fear, and paranoia, yet at the same time dominated by a remarkable egoism'. He believed that

48

German statesmen and soldiers by the second decade of the twentieth century could see escape from their predicament only in a 'mad bolt'. That this encirclement had been largely self-imposed and that it could have been overcome easily by a peaceful foreign policy apparently never dawned on the planners in Berlin, absorbed as many of them were in social Darwinistic and deterministic visions of the rise and fall of world empires.

The publication of the diaries of Kurt Riezler, Bethmann-Hollweg's closest adviser, in 1972, only served to reinforce this view of the German leadership being fully prepared to pursue a dangerous, high-risk strategy in 1914, though there remained some disagreement over whether this was to further long-nurtured aggressive designs or because of defensive motives.

Analysis of the origins of the First World War has therefore been profoundly influenced by the 'Fischer revolution'; by the mid-1980s, Fischer's interpretation of German policy had become accepted as the new orthodoxy. Writing in *Europe Transformed* in 1983, Norman Stone, Regius Professor of History at Oxford commented, 'not many historians nowadays dissent from the proposition that the German government egged on by its generals deliberately provoked the war of 1914'. John Moses in *The Politics of Illusion* (1975) says that most critics of Fischer 'now accept his view that Germany deliberately unleashed the First World War' though there is still argument about the extent to which the German government was actually planning for war before 1914. Fischer claimed that the 'central truth' was that 'in July 1914 a will to war existed solely and alone on the German side and that all arrangements on the side of the Entente served the defensive security of their alliance. And this will to war had been crystallising for many years previously.' Some historians, while not disputing this, have emphasized the opportunistic nature of German policy in taking advantage of the favourable circumstances of 1914 and are less convinced that Germany had actually been deliberately planning for war before 1912. James Joll, in *The Origins of the First World War* (1984), argued that by December 1912 German rulers had 'accepted war as inevitable' but were concerned to wage it at the most opportune time. The relative decline of Austrian military power as a result of the Balkan wars, the steady growth of Russian military and industrial power and the completion of the widening of the Kiel Canal to enable it to accommodate the passage of the German battle fleet from the Baltic to the North Sea, all combined to suggest July 1914 as the 'moment of destiny'.

Herwig, in a chapter entitled 'Industry, Empire and the First World War', in *Modern Germany Reconsidered* (Martel (ed.) 1992), suggests that three-quarters of Fischer's assertions are now accepted as valid. However, disagreements remain, largely over the importance of the 'war council' meeting of December 1912 and of the extent to which it supports the view that Germany was planning for war since that time. According to John Röhl, writing about German policy in the excellent volume *Decisions for War, 1914* (1995) edited by Keith Wilson, 'the exciting hypothesis is gaining ground, as previously hidden sources come to light, that the decision was taken not in response to the Sarajevo assassination, but some time before that event took place, as a result of a long process which began in earnest with Germany's perceived humiliation in the Second Morocco Crisis'. Thus for Rohl, the 'war council' meeting was an important stage in the unfolding of German plans to prepare for war against the *entente* powers at the earliest favourable opportunity. David Stevenson takes a more measured view, arguing in *Armaments and the Coming of War* that 'the principal significance of the 8 December meeting . . . was in heightening Germany's medium term preparedness'. He points out that those at the meeting 'rejected an early war' and that the war council was followed by little increase in 'immediate readiness'. Niall Ferguson expands upon this interpretation in his challenging revisionist work *The Pity of War* (1999), asserting that 'the so-called "war council" of military chiefs summoned by the Kaiser in December 1912 was really nothing of the kind'. Although Moltke argued for 'war, the sooner the better', Tirpitz asked for another eighteen months because his navy was not yet ready. Ferguson adds that the result of the meeting, as Admiral Müller noted in his diary, was 'pretty well zero'.

So to what extent did a strong 'will to war' exist amongst German leaders in the years before 1914, and did the crisis sparked off by the Sarajevo assassinations offer them the opportunity of a 'grab at world power' or alternatively the chance to secure political and economic hegemony over central and eastern Europe? Were their policies the product of confident, determined, military expansionism, as argued by Pogge von Strandmann in *The Coming of the First World War* (1991)? Did the Germans seize the opportunity of the assassination crisis, as Röhl suggests, to strengthen their European position by launching 'a lightning attack on France and Russia in the very near future before they became too strong and Austria-Hungary too weak'? Or was German policy fuelled instead by growing pessimism and despair?

Niall Ferguson has argued very convincingly in his recent book, *The Pity of War,* that what weighed most heavily with German leaders, and especially the General Staff, by the summer of 1914 were 'pessimistic calculations about the relative present and future strengths of the European armies'. As the Kaiser acknowledged in early July, 'Russia is at the present moment militarily and financially totally unprepared for war'. But military leaders warned that once the Russians had completed their strategic railroads in Poland, 'our position will be untenable'. In a few years' time, Russia could 'crush us by the number of soldiers; then she will have built her Baltic Sea Fleet and her strategic railroads'. The case for a pre-emptive strike, arising from the opportunity offered by the growing crisis between Austria and Serbia which Russia could hardly ignore, was argued most forcefully by the Chief of the General Staff von Moltke when he warned, 'We shall never again strike as well as we do now, with France's and Russia's expansion of their armies incomplete'. Chancellor Bethmann-Hollweg acknowledged the compelling logic of a preventive war, agreeing that 'if war must break out, better now than in one or two years' time when the Entente will be stronger'.

The argument that German leaders, in the summer of 1914, were willing and even eager to wage a 'preventive war' on the *entente* powers, if they were not prepared to stand by and watch Austria crush Serbia, is supported by the recent work of David Stevenson and David Herrman. Both authors refer to the 'window of opportunity' which opened up for Germany after 1912, as a result of the massive peace time expansion of the German army. This was prompted by Russian military recovery and reorganisation which took place after 1910, by the growing realisation that in a future conflict Germany would be faced not just by France as an enemy but by Russia and Britain as well and by the growing evidence that Germany had lost her naval race with Britain. If drastic measures were not taken quickly, the military balance on the European continent would tip decisively against her as well.

Inevitably the German programmes of military expansion pro-voked strong reactions from France and from Russia. Within four or

51

five years, Russia would be able to mobilise a massive army more quickly than she had ever been able to do before. France was modernising her military equipment and responded to the German challenge by passing a law to lengthen the term of compulsory military service to three years, though this would not boost army strength significantly until 1915–16. And relations between Britain and France, and even more alarmingly from Germany's perspective, between Britain and Russia, became ever closer. The prospect of encirclement seemed real enough to large numbers of Germans, and fear of the westward spread of Russian power was widespread and strong. It would not be difficult for German leaders to win general public support for a military conflict with Russia, and the circumstances of June and July of 1914 offered the ideal opportunity for a German army at the peak of its strength and power to challenge the military forces of the *entente* powers.

The dangers of competing power blocs

However, the work of both Herrman and of Stevenson does not just focus on German ambitions and policies between 1912 and 1914, but lays emphasis on the extent to which successive diplomatic crises after 1906 increased military preparedness amongst the European powers and tightened the links within the emerging power blocs. After 1912, their detailed researches show how calculations of military strength and of the balance of military advantage became a dominant factor influencing decision making in cabinets and councils across Europe. To some extent, their work recalls inter-war critiques, which blamed the outbreak of war on the existence in Europe of ever more powerful and rigid alliance systems and on a spiralling arms race. Both authors reveal in great detail how the escalation of tension after the first Moroccan crisis of 1906 and the calculations of the military strength of the different alignments of powers generated by each successive crisis shaped the perceptions and policies of rival blocs. Herrman lays particular emphasis on the recovery of Russian strength after 1910, and the Balkan rivalries and wars of 1912–13, which saw the elimination of Turkey 'as a counterweight to the Balkan states in south eastern Europe' and the emergence of Serbia and Montenegro to pose a wholly new and dangerous military threat to Austria-Hungary. The interplay of crises, of the growth of armaments, and of military confrontations in south eastern Europe increased expectations in many quarters by the end of 1913 that war was inevitable.

There was undoubtedly a contemporary perception of an arms race which fuelled tensions, even though by modern standards, levels of spending on armaments were relatively low, compared, say, to the late 1930s or to the height of the Cold War in the 1950s and 60s. As Stevenson points out, though bare statistics show spending on armaments in the pre 1914 period to have been fairly modest, the costs were borne by much poorer societies than in later years, and military and naval budgets normally accounted for the majority of government spending and taxation. In addition, the so-called 'arms race' was actually a multiple phenomenon, involving not just the two power blocs, but the spiralling tensions amongst Balkan powers and Austria-Hungary as well.

Ferguson's calculations support the view that the amounts of money being spent by the major European powers on armaments before 1914, whilst steadily rising, were not excessive. However, the growing problem, he argues, was financing the arms bill, and the political problems this caused for all countries but particularly for Germany. Attempts to modernise and to centralise the fiscal system and to increase taxes caused a political outcry on the part of entrenched and influential groups, leading to severe frustration in government and military circles. Britain was winning the naval race because, as shipping magnate Albert Ballin lamented, 'we just cannot afford a race in dreadnoughts against the much wealthier British'. And the same inability to raise the necessary resources was now threatening army expansion, according to von Moltke in late 1912, when he warned, 'Our enemies are arming more vigorously than we, because we are strapped for cash'. Domestic and political constraints on financial reform, it seemed, were so strong that Germany was doomed in the longer term to lose the financial arms race. Here was perhaps another reason for seeking an early military confrontation rather than watching helplessly as Germany's rivals built up their military strength. As we have already seen, a war against Russia was likely to be popular and to win strong backing and financial resources, on the part of nearly all deputies in the *Reichstag*.

How significant a factor were domestic tensions?

Some historians have argued that it was not just in Germany that pre-industrial elites saw war as the only way of resolving internal tensions and maintaining their position. Arno Mayer in *The Persistence of the Old Regime* (1981) presented a picture of general crisis 'in the politics and policy of Europe's ruling and governing classes', not just in Germany but in other major countries as well. In the past two decades, therefore, much work has been carried out on the pre-war planning and domestic situations of the other major European states. Historians have examined a considerable amount of archival and primary source material in Austria-Hungary, France, Britain, Russia, Serbia and Italy to see whether and to what extent internal considerations affected the foreign policy decision-making of the ruling elites in these countries.

In Austria-Hungary there was clearly a sense of desperation at the intractable internal and external problems facing the Habsburg dynasty, and military action, rather than diplomacy, seemed to be the best way to deal with them. By the end of 1913, the majority of ministers wanted to solve the Serbian problem by force. Samuel Williamson, in *Austria-Hungary and the Origins of the First World War* (1991), has shown that the policy-makers in Vienna pursued a consistently belligerent policy in 1914 and that there was a fateful meshing of 'aggressive German *Weltpolitik*' with an even more aggressive, irresponsible 'Habsburg *Balkanpolitik*'. But in Russia, while it was accepted that a strong foreign policy could arouse enthusiasm and command support amongst large sections of the population, it was feared that involvement in war itself could give rise to social disorders and revolution. Careful studies of the policies pursued by Russia, France and Britain before 1914 have revealed that domestic considerations were as likely to have acted as a brake on an aggressive foreign policy as to have promoted one. As Michael Howard has argued, in *The Outbreak of World War I* (edited by Holger Herwig, 1997) rather than war being seen as a panacea for social ills, 'the opposite was likely to have been the case, because governments were far from certain what impact war would have domestically.' In France there was considerable opposition to the three-year conscription law and a strong campaign had been launched by left-wing and centre parties to change it back to two years. Agitation to win back Alsace and Lorraine had completely subsided and the fate of the 'Lost Provinces' was no longer considered a live political issue. Studies which have attempted to analyse French public opinion in 1914 have concluded that the overall mood was one of profound pacifism and of consuming interest in domestic issues. In Britain, the violent tactics of the suffragettes and the disorders in the north of Ireland were a serious challenge to the Liberal government, which had no wish to become embroiled at the same time in crisis abroad. Even in the Habsburg Empire, Magyar leaders were not happy at the prospect of large numbers of Slavs being incorporated into the empire and tried in July 1914 to slow down the pace of decisions which would result in a war with Serbia.

Historians now agree that there was no deliberate desire on the part of Russia or France to engage in war before 1914; these states acted defensively to protect what they regarded as vital national interests and would have preferred to protect them without resort to war. Even in Serbia the government was not a party to the recruiting and training of conspirators, which was master-minded in secrecy by the chief of Serbian military intelligence, Colonel Dimitrijevic. When the Serb government found out about the assassination attempt, through a report filed by one of its agents in early June, it tried, albeit ineffectively, to forestall it and to warn the Habsburg government of what was afoot.

Writing in *Russia and the Origins of the First World War* (1983), Dominic Lieven concluded that 'study of the July crisis from the Russian standpoint . . . confirms the now generally accepted view that the major immediate responsibility for the outbreak of war rested unequivocally on the German government'. More recently, Pogge von Strandmann has asserted that 'in the present state of research, the evidence that Germany and Austria started the war and dragged the rest of the powers into it is even stronger than in the early 1960s when Fischer published his analysis of German war aims policies'. He believes that the studies of all the major European powers before 1914 clearly show that the view that Germany 'fought a defensive war' is untenable, and the picture of all nations slithering 'over the brink' is unconvincing. There was no general 'drift into war' in 1914; rather there was 'the determination of one power to exploit the Balkan crisis to change the international status quo in its favour'.

The mood in Europe before 1914

In recent years, historians have drawn attention to the general European climate of ideas and philosophies which influenced and shaped the thinking of civilian and military leaders and the responses of their populations. The atmosphere throughout Europe in 1914 promoted a war mentality, and declarations of war generated great excitement in the different European capitals. In August 1914, young men clamoured to be called up. War was regarded not just in Germany but in Britain, France and Russia as offering a colourful escape from a dull existence, as giving opportunities for individual heroism and for acts of defiant bravery. Throughout Europe in the decades before 1914, education had spread and with it came the opportunity for governments to instil notions of nationalism, of the glorious past and of dreams for future greatness. Higher levels of literacy led to the growth of a popular press and of romantic escapist fiction. War was popularized in such literature as a positive force which could promote discipline, loyalty and comradeship. Young boys read epic tales about heroic deeds on the north-west frontier, about fights in the jungle to spread civilization and Christianity, and about frontier battles with Indians of the wild west. Intrepid adventurers and traders fired the imagination with their successes against native populations and the vast extent of their territorial annexations. Governments were drawn in to the protection of trading routes and territories and to the denial of access to nationals of other countries. As more and more young men served a military apprenticeship in Europe before 1914, army leaders and trainers took the opportunity to instil into them codes of military honour and notions of the glorious opportunities that war offered to overcome individual concerns and self interest and to display bravery and courage.

At the same time the popular press was jingoistic in its tone and was quick to promote the interests of the home government in the face of foreign challenges. Theories of evolution and popular notions about the survival of the fittest spilled over into nationalist thinking. Countries needed to expand their influence or they would decline. White nations had to bring enlightenment to Zulus, Hindus and Chinamen, and power over non-European peoples added to prestige and status as against other great powers. There was keen competition amongst all the European great powers for influence and for domination in the wider world, for political as well as economic motives.

Great powers were acutely conscious of the need to preserve and to enhance their position and their status, and this fuelled tensions in many parts of the world, as John Lowe has shown so clearly in *The Great Powers, Imperialism and the German Problem, 1865–1925* (1994). As Lord Curzon, British Viceroy in India and later foreign secretary, commented in 1901, 'if we lose [India] we shall drop straight away to a third rate power'. And the consequences of such a catastrophic loss of great power status were too frightening to contemplate.

While such considerations were an important element in the external policies of individual countries, there were also contrary pressures at work – anti-war and anti-imperialist sentiments voiced by individuals and by groups of trade unionists and intellectuals, and a growing belief amongst liberals everywhere that international disputes should be regulated by arbitration and peaceful means. The meetings of the Second International of socialist parties and the two Hague Conferences of 1899 and 1907 show the strength of such currents. Furthermore, the fact that some socialists, such as Lenin and many of the members of the Social Democratic Party in Germany, looked forward to war (especially involving Russia) as a necessary prelude to revolution and progress towards communism, was likely to act as a brake on aggressive action by some governments and political leaders.

Some accounts of the origins of the war have stressed the industrial and technological developments of the late-nineteenth century and the important consequences that these had for military calculations. The increasingly mechanized nature of warfare, the importance of railway transport, the ability to mobilize greater and greater numbers of men quickly and to arm them with rapid-firing guns seemed to point to the supreme importance of seizing the initiative in a crisis which was going to erupt into war. This belief in the importance of an early preemptive strike went hand in hand with an ideological preference in most European countries for the offensive military strategy as giving the greatest opportunities for a successful display of national spirit. Taylor has referred to 'war by timetable' in 1914 and there is no doubt that the need for the Germans to capture Liège and transport large numbers of troops through Belgium as rapidly as possible was an important factor influencing the calculations and the actions of the German government in late July. The French and Russian military authorities were also obsessed by the importance of a rapid offensive and were concerned not to be taken by surprise and caught napping by the military preparations of their enemies.

57

Recent investigations have revealed that European governments were well aware of the general nature of the military plans of their opponents. *Knowing One's Enemies* gives us a fascinating picture of the exchange of intelligence in Europe before 1914 and the extent to which countries had penetrated the secret codes and military plans of their neighbours. And yet rather than change their own strategies to thwart the intentions of their enemies, they used the information they received to justify their existing strategies and to argue that there was no reasonable alternative to their proposed course of action. It was clearly not secret diplomacy in itself which caused war in 1914; indeed, secret intelligence gave governments the opportunity to avoid war and to put pressure on their rivals to negotiate differences or to prepare to meet the military challenges of their opponents so effectively that war was not worth contemplating.

Thus one is left with the strong impression that what really marked out the decade before 1914 was a failure of statesmanship and of hope. By 1912, most European governments had come to believe that a general European war was inevitable and that the problems which plagued them both at home and abroad could no longer be settled by negotiation and by diplomacy. Austria-Hungary did not believe that the threat posed by Serbian ambitions could be totally removed by any means other than war. The Russian government assumed that continuing Turkish decline would unleash a struggle for influence in the Near East in which Russian leaders would have to be prepared to seize Constantinople by force. Diplomatic action alone would not suffice to protect Russia's vital interests in the face of belligerent German and Austro-Hungarian pressure. Equally, Serbia would have to be supported by military assistance in the face of an Austro-Hungarian attack. Russia was not prepared to see the Balkans domin-ated by an Austro-Hungarian–German 'bloc', and again, diplomatic support alone in the circumstances of 1914 was not considered a sufficiently strong response.

German leaders saw their hopes of European domination and world power status being threatened by a declining Austria-Hungary and a rapidly industrializing Russia. The idea of a preventive war against Russia grew very attractive after 1912 and clearly dominated military thinking in Berlin in the summer crisis of 1914. It was not so much that German leaders had laid plans for a major war as that they believed that sooner or later Germany would have to fight to survive and to expand as a major power. The only alternative to expansion was seen to be national decline. July 1914, before France and Russia had completed their programmes of military expansion, seemed to offer the best prospects for a successful outcome. The use of force to break diplomatic deadlocks both at home and abroad was not a new concept in German thinking. Bismarck had employed it most successfully in 1866 against the Austrian Empire and in 1870 against France. The result had been the establishment of a solidly autocratic unified Germany, the decline of the power of the German liberals and a dramatic expansion in economic power since 1871. Now the consequences of that economic growth were causing problems and the pursuit of *Junker* objectives both at home and abroad was becoming blocked. It was hardly surprising that in these circumstances war seemed to offer an attractive way out, a solution to both domestic and foreign antagonisms. And if that war could be made appealing to all sections of the population – as a war against Tsarist Russia most certainly would be, even to ardent socialists – then so much the better. There can be no doubt at all that German leaders were prepared for war in 1914 and exploited the crisis of June–July 1914 to bring it about.

While there was no such positive wish to wage war in France or in Britain, both powers believed their national interests to be threatened by the actions of Germany and Austria-Hungary in 1914. Neither power was prepared to see German domination of Europe, and their entry into the conflict was in no way the result of accident or miscalculation. Just as the Germans sought to increase their power, so Britain and France sought to contain it, by military means if necessary. In this sense it could be argued that both powers fought to try to restore the balance of power to Europe.

Countries went to war because they believed that they could achieve more through war than by diplomatic negotiation and that if they stood aside their status as great powers would be gravely affected. That was their greatest miscalculation. The balance sheet in 1918 proved how wrong they had been; by that time the status of all Europe's major powers had been greatly diminished and virtually none of the objectives of the European ruling élites had been realized.

Annotated select bibliography

Place of publication is London unless otherwise stated.

General accounts

E. R. Bridge, *The Coming of the First World War* (1983) Compact Historical Association pamphlet

R. J. Evans and H. Pogge von Strandmann, *The Coming of the First World War* (Oxford, 1991) Useful book, which takes a country by country approach

Niall Ferguson, *The Pity of War* (1999) A readable, lively, sometimes controversial but very comprehensive reassessment of the origins, course and impact of the war

David Herrman, *The Arming of Europe and the Making of the First World War* (Princeton, U.S.A., 1996) An excellent analysis of the growth of armaments, escalation of crises and European rivalries between 1904 and 1914

Holger Herwig (ed), *The Outbreak of World War I* (U.S.A., 1997) A collection of writings on the origins of the war, covering a wide range of interpretations

James Joll, *The Origins of the First World War* (1984) A very good starting point for students wanting to explore in greater depth the central issues involved

L. Lafore, *The Long Fuse* (New York, 1973)

R. Langhorne, *The Collapse of the Concert of Europe (1981)* Succinct account of the unfolding diplomatic and international crises from the late 19th century onwards

J. Lowe, *The Great Powers, Imperialism and the German Problem, 1865–1925* (1994) A broad introductory study which looks at economic and political rivalries in a global context

B. Schmitt, *The Origins of the First World War* (1958) A rather dated but still useful pamphlet

David Stevenson, *Armaments and the Coming of War* (Oxford, 1996) Comprehensive reappraisal of pre-war drift to militarised diplomacy and the rise of an inter-bloc armaments competition

A. J. P. Taylor, *The Struggle for Mastery in Europe 1848–1918* (1954) Highly-readable and still classic survey of European diplomatic history in the 19th and early 20th centuries

L. C. F. Turner, *The Origins of the First World War* (New York, 1967)

Keith Wilson (ed) *Decisions for War, 1914* (1995) Excellent collection of contributions, on a country by country basis

Books on individual countries

V. R. Berghahn, *Germany and the Approach of War in 1914* (1973)

F. R. Bridge, *From Sadowa to Sarajevo* (1972) An assessment of 19th and early 20th century Habsburg diplomacy

J. Keiger, *France and the Origins of the First World War* (1983)

D. C. B. Lieven, *Russia and the Origins of the First World War* (1983)

G. Martel (ed), *Modern Germany Reconsidered* (1992) Contains an interesting chapter on 'Industry, Empire and the First World War' by Holger Herwig

J. W. Mason, *The Dissolution of the Austro-Hungarian Empire* (1985)

Z. S. Steiner, *Britain and the Origins of the First World War* (1977) Standard account of Britain's approach to the coming of war, somewhat at odds with Ferguson's interpretation

S. Williamson, *Austria-Hungary and the Origins of the First World War* (1991)

Index